6/1/2007

The Olive and the Tree

To Denise

best wishes!

Dr. Ruth

Westheimer

D1526246

green press INITIATIVE

The Olive and the Tree

The Secret Strength of the Druze

Dr. Ruth K. Westheimer
and Gil Sedan

Lantern Books · New York

A Division of Booklight Inc.

2007
Lantern Books
One Union Square West, Suite 201
New York, NY 10003

Printed in Canada.

Library of Congress Cataloging-in-Publication Data

Westheimer, Ruth.
  The olive and the tree : the secret strength of the Druze / Ruth Westheimer, Gil Sedan.
    p. cm.
  ISBN-13: 978-1-59056-102-7 (alk. paper)
  ISBN-10: 1-59056-102-3 (alk. paper)
  1. Druzes. I. Sedan, Gil. II. Title.
  BL1695.W47 2007
  297.8'5—dc22
                                    2006101667

"The strangers who sojourn with you shall be to you as the natives among you, and you shall love them as yourself; for you were strangers in the land of Egypt."

LEVITICUS 19:33–34

DEDICATION

To the memory of my entire family who perished during the Holocaust—I am thankful that they had the opportunity to instill in me the much-cherished values of the Jewish Tradition before they were lost to me. And to the memory of my beloved late husband Manfred Westheimer, and to the memory of Henry Everett.

To my wonderful family of now: my daughter Miriam Westheimer, Ed.D; my son-in-law, Joel Einleger, MBA; my grandson, Ari Einleger; my granddaughter, Leora Einleger; my son, Joel Westheimer, Ph.D.; my daughter-in-law, Barbara Leckie, Ph.D.; my granddaughter, Michal Westheimer Leckie; and my grandson, Benjamin Manfred Westheimer!

Table of Contents

Acknowledgments

This book is not a historical survey, nor is it a political or sociological study. It is more of a snapshot of who the Druze, a relatively unknown community in Israel, are today based on a month-long journey I made in the summer of 2005.

This is not a journey that I could have made by myself. Since I was shooting a documentary, I am of course most grateful to my crew, with whom I have worked before: producer/director Michael Greenspan, camera operator Colin Rosen, and sound engineer Yoni Lubliner.

Because the Druze are a closed community, my crew and I would have ended up spending that month wandering lost in the desert if it hadn't been for one man, my coauthor of this book, Gil Sedan. Gil is a respected Israeli journalist and, most important, respected by the Druze. He was able to act as our guide and to open many doors that not only would have been closed to us, but also would have been invisible in the first place. Gil continued the exploration even after I was gone, and what he found fills many pages of this book.

While making the documentary, our team toured the Druze villages of Israel, and the wonderful people we met acted as our guides. They were from all walks of Druze life, and if they hadn't taken us by the hand, we might have been like so many tourists who touch only the surface of Druze life and never get to peer inside the tent to see what really goes on.

It is, therefore, our pleasure to thank our guides in this illuminating tour: Ali Birani, Salman Natour, Samih Natour and Amal Nasser a-Din of Daliat al-Carmel, Professor Fadel Mansour, Najwa and Ghassan Mansour of Issfiya, Dr. Janan Falah and her husband Iyyad Faraj of Acre, Savta Jamila and her son Fuad of Peki'in, Zaki, Wissam Irahim of Sajour, Riad Ali of Mughar and Cindy Offenbacher and Akivah Offenbacher, Ph.D.

Special thanks to Dr. Nissim Dana and Dr. Shimon Avivi, two of the leading experts on the Druze community in Israel, who contributed their unique "Jewish" perspective on their Druze friends and neighbors. Their writings have been invaluable in creating the historical and sociological background to our discoveries.

Unlike most of my books, this one would never have come together if there had not first been a documentary. Moreover, without the generous contributions of so many, the documentary would never have been filmed. So the first group I want to acknowledge are those generous individuals and foundations who contributed to the making of the documentary: The Everett Foundation, Ronald Lauder, Fema and Nily Falic, Connie and Harvey Krueger, The Judy and Michael Steinhardt Foundation, The Theodore and Renee Weiler Foundation, The Alan B. Slivka Foundation, The Andrea and Charles Bronfman Fund, The Alan C. Greenberg Philanthropic Foundation, Semone Grossman, Peter Joseph and Elizabeth Scheuer, The Zolla Family Foundation, The Herbert & Caryl Ackerman Philanthropic Foundation, Sylvia Hassenfeld, The Dennis & Brooks Holt Foundation and Howard Schur. I also must thank Victor Ganzi and the Hearst Corporation for their generous contribution towards educating Americans about the Druze through this book.

Then must come those who were part of the labor of love that creating this documentary was, most especially Michael Greenspan, who shared executive producer credit with me, wrote the script, directed the filming, and did the narration. Next is Colin Rosen, who produced the film and was our director of photography. Then there's our editor Hanita Admony-Atoun, sound people Yoni Lubliner and Misha Spektor, mixer Kobi Eisenmann, graphic designer Maya Agassi, and on-line editor Aviran Aldema.

While all the filming took place in Israel, much crucial work took place in New York. Amir Shaviv and The Joint Distribution Committee were instrumental in getting me started and offering their services throughout the course of production. Cliff Rubin, as my special assistant kept me organized, no small task. And Pierre Lehu, my Minister of Communications, contributed in so many ways, both in the making of the film and the book, that without him, I don't know if either would have come to pass.

Finally, there's my coauthor of this book, Gil Sedan. Gil's title on the film is Consultant and Researcher, but that barely scratches the surface of what he did. Without his contacts among the Druze community, we might have remained outsiders looking in, which would have made for a very different film. Instead we were welcomed among the Druze and so were able to give a much more insightful and detailed picture of these amazing people. And not only did Gil do a yeoman's job on this book, but some of his work was done under difficult conditions. Gil, thank you, thank you, thank you.

Dr. Ruth at a Galilee hilltop at filming location.

INTRODUCTION

Many novelists write about what they know, especially in a first novel. The characters' experiences are often related directly to what the author experienced at an earlier age. I've never had the urge to write fiction; real life fascinates me far too much for that. In my exploration of the real world, however, in both literary and film documentary form, I have followed a theme that stems from my own experiences in this world, which is basically what happens to a child during the formative years; the core values passed on by parents build a foundation that carries children through whatever this world might throw at them later on.

The first group I studied was the young Jewish-Germans who had been with me at the children's home in Heiden, Switzerland. They had been sent there to escape the Nazis, and all became orphans. I followed that study with one on what happened to the Ethiopian Jews who went from a primitive culture to modern-day Israel. I also made documentaries on how grandmothers kept religious values alive in Russia under communism, as well as on the peoples of the Trobriand Islands. In this book and in its companion documentary, I've chosen a little known group of people from the Middle East: the Druze.

I've written many "how-to" books, but the lessons I learned from the Druze, which I want to pass on to you, are not related to the subject for which I am best known. Instead, the Druze show us how much of an impact families can have on their children, even against seemingly insurmountable odds.

Every religion offers its adherents keys to living a better life, but the Druze perspective is particularly interesting to outside observers, because they have developed a special "art" of adjustment that encompasses all of life—religious and nonreligious, the old and the young, women and children.

One key element that may help you understand how this works is their ancient custom of *a-takkiya* (preservation); it means that, in time of communal stress, the Druze minimize their religious identity, refrain from accentuating it, and at times even pretend to practice the religion of the majority in the society. This is why the Druze in Israel are loyal to the state of Israel, while the Druze in Syria, Israel's adversary, are loyal to that country. The Druze fought alongside the Mamluks against the Mongols, then sided with the Ottoman Turks against the Mamluks. Today, one can find Druze soldiers in the Israeli Defense Forces (IDF), as well as in the Arab armies across the border from Israel.

So, you see that, although the Druze are considered a very brave and proud group of people, they differ from other peoples and religions in that they avoid unnecessary confrontations with their neighbors and focus their efforts instead on building their society as they see fit.

The primary aim of the Druze is to build themselves up as individuals, both for their own benefit and for the Druze "tribe," according to Professor Fadel Mansour of the village of Issfiya near Haifa. He was one of many who opened the door for us to that fascinating community. This, he says, is a continuous mission, from birth until death—and after. "After death" because, according to Druze beliefs, a Druze person never really dies. The Druze soul is transformed into the body of another

Druze, thus family bonds are stronger than in the typical nuclear family. The Druze regard themselves as one big family.

Ethnically, the Druze are Arab (though often throughout history they have undergone bitter, sometimes bloody, conflicts with their Arab brethren). Most Druze live in a particular part of the world, and that little piece of geography happens to lie within the borders of three separate countries: Lebanon, Syria, and Israel. Given the state of conflict among those host countries, it's easy to see why the art of *a-takkiya* would come in handy. Much of the information in this book about the Druze encompasses all three areas, but for first-hand information I limited my studies to those Druze living in Israel. Access to the others would have been difficult for this little Jew. The Druze who live in Israel, however, face another set of problems. Whereas the Druze are a minority within the Muslim majority throughout the Middle East, in Israel they are a minority within a minority, which makes life even more complicated.

How do they cope with this situation? First, by sticking to their villages, which are located within breathtaking scenery on top of the Galilee and Carmel mountains; second, by taking part inside the "holy of the holies" of Israeli society—the defense forces—thus integrating fully into the majority. There is a catch to this second aspect; military service exposes the young Druze men to temptations of the outside Western world. Not that this is negative per se, but it has the dangerous potential of leading to assimilation, thus losing their special Druze heritage. The society must be strong enough to deter young Druze men and women from leaving the community and joining the outside, Western-oriented Jewish world. It must make sure that the Druze youth return home. The only way to do this is to ensure that the family is stronger than outside temptations. The only way to accomplish this is for the

Druze to educate their young people in an agreed-upon set of codes and rules. The ultimate manifestation of that codex is the day when a Druze woman brings her children to the bond of marriage, for a Druze must marry another Druze to remain Druze. Thus, children who have made it to that point can be considered truly Druze.

Although Druze tradition is patriarchal, the Druze woman has a special status in the family. Not only is she the *only* wife, unlike Muslim tradition, she is also equal to the husband in practice.

The Druze response to the question "How does one make the best of one's life?" is not foolproof; it is constantly challenged by the outside world and sometimes lacks the strength to cope with it. In recent years, Druze villages have suffered the ravages of drugs and youth delinquency. Druze society must fight those dangerous developments, because it cannot afford to lose members to any form of temptation. If the Druze community shrinks too much, it will pass a tipping point that leads to extinction. To fight these assaults, it must cooperate with Israeli authorities, exposing its dirty laundry, which has been anathema to the Druze since their origins.

Despite Israeli Jews' love of traveling the world to explore new societies, the Druze fight for their identity has been ignored by their next-door neighbors. Yet ask the Jewish residents of Haifa about the inhabitants of Daliat al-Carmel, a mere twenty-minute drive away, and they will be unable to answer such basic questions as: Who are the Druze? What is their history? What does their religion stand for? What current problems do they face?

As we visited Daliat al-Carmel one Saturday afternoon, rubbing elbows with the scores of Israeli Jews who filled the village's main street and restaurants, we conducted short street interviews. When we asked the tourists what they knew about their hosts, they gave these answers: "We love the atmosphere here—their food, their attitude; they are very nice." "They are part of us, they do army service, and they give to the country." "They devote themselves totally to Israel; they are great."

Israeli Jews *think* they know the Druze, but actually they don't. They delude themselves that, if they make an occasional trip to a Druze village, sit in a local restaurant, enjoy the humus, and shop for "authentic" Druze goods, they have opened themselves up to the Druze society.

Gil Sedan has been covering the Druze community as a television reporter for almost thirty years, and, following our research for the documentary and this book, only now does he realize how much he didn't know about them.

Druze society is very complex; friendly, yet sometimes violent; reaching out, yet closed to outsiders; divided and, at the same time, unified; ethnically Arab, but sometimes with a stronger Zionist conviction than the Jews; traditional, but uncertain of its identity. All these contradictions make the Druze society both fascinating and difficult to understand.

WHO ARE THE DRUZE?

THE DRUZE PAID DEARLY FOR violating a very basic tenet of life: Religions do not tolerate deviations from the main track. Sometime in the eleventh century they offered a new, quite daring interpretation of Islam, which infuriated mainstream Islamists. A clash with the new splinter group was inevitable. Relations with the mother religion (which itself is split into Sunni and Shiite sects) have been sour ever since. This may provide one explanation of why, in Israel at least, they get along better with the Jews than with the Palestinian Arabs, their ethnic brethren.

The Druze "homeland" lies in the mountainous regions of Lebanon, Syria, and Israel. Historically, they were farmers who terraced the mountainsides with soil brought from riverbeds. At the same time, they clung to their swords and acquired a reputation as fearless warriors. Only in the past fifty years or so have many of them moved to urban professions, particularly in Israel.

The Druze are negligible in terms of absolute numbers, with only about 1.2 million in the entire world, about 600,000 live in Syria, 400,000 in Lebanon, and 115,000 in Israel. Small Druze émigré communities live in Jordan, Saudi Arabia, the Americas, Australia, and even the Philippines. In Israel they are a minority within a minority, making up about 1.6 percent of the general population of seven million.

The Druze call themselves *muwahhidun*, or "monotheists." Not that they ignore Abraham's contribution to monotheism, but, after all, they believe, they were here first. According to the Druze creed, they have been here since the creation and have believed in one God since day one, while throughout history they remained behind the scenes, modestly contributing to the human body of knowledge. With all due respect to Judaism, Christianity, and Islam, the Druze believe that those other religions revealed only *part* of the Divine truth. Not that they had something to hide, but the Druze religion remained hidden because the "circumstances were not fitting." The "right circumstances" were formed only in the eleventh century, during the reign of the Fatimid Khalif al-Hakim bi'Amerillah in Egypt, when the Druze disciples could finally expose their belief to the world and split from the Shia sect of Islam.

For now, let us leave the details of Druze history aside, so that we can dig right in to our prime story: the Druze community in Israel.

* * *

The Druze had already settled in the Galilee area in the early days of their religion, in the eleventh century. Nonetheless, the Druze villages in the Carmel are relatively new. They were founded after the Ottoman army defeated the forces of the Druze prince Fakhr a-Din II in 1633, following internal struggles between the Druze in Lebanon. They were later joined by Druze from Halab in Syria. They did not remain in the Carmel region for long, however, because of the heavy taxes imposed by the Ottoman authorities, conscription to the Turkish army, and the overall hostility by the authorities and their Muslim neighbors. Many Druze ended up leaving their lands in the Carmel and emigrating to the Horan in Syria.

The Druze's ability to survive is one trait they have in common with the Jews. Like the Jews, solidarity with the tribe has often been paramount, surmounting any other loyalty. Like the Jews, they have had their share of bitter internal strife, but never strong enough to break the communal bond. Preserving the community and maintaining its strength have always been prime elements in the history of the Druze.

The Druze are not a tribal society in the Bedouin, African, or Native American sense of the term. Beyond the immediate family, there is the enlarged family—the *Hamula*. The Druze community as a whole is a "federation" of Hamulas. The family is the core of the community, one of the main factors contributing to its preservation. It derives its power from both the individuals who comprise it and from the community made up of the families. Any insult to the family may be interpreted as a slap to the entire community.

One of the main pillars of the Druze religion is mutual, brotherly aid. *Hafth al-Ikhwan* or "guarding the brothers," compels Druze individuals to express solidarity with their people during times of stress to protect their rights, their property, and their honor. This Druze solidarity crosses borders and may take place because of their loyalty to the local authorities. We will see how Druze brides from the Israeli-controlled Golan Heights cross the border to Syria, to marry Syrian Druze. When Lebanese Druze felt threatened by their Christian neighbors, Israeli Druze rallied to their support, forcing the Israeli government to take a more pro-Druze policy in Lebanon.

Druze in one village will raise funds to help a needy family in another village. Thus, a Druze individual will never stand alone to face the hardships of life. The immediate family, and if necessary, the entire clan, village, or community, will stand with and help the individual.

Although loyalty to the community can surpass loyalty to

the state, the Druze will avoid confrontation with the state without an explicit decision by the community to do so. Thus, for example, during a conflict with the Golan Druze over Israel's decision to impose Israeli law in the Golan, Israeli Druze as a community tried to stay out of the conflict. Nevertheless, many Druze have spoken out publicly against the Israeli government's position vis-à-vis the Golan Druze.

Historically, the Druze settled in remote and protected mountainous regions, as far as possible from the reach of the central government, in an attempt to enjoy as much autonomy as they could. Nevertheless, throughout their long history, the Druze have never achieved political independence but accepted foreign rule as long as their basic rights were preserved. They enjoyed a fair measure of autonomy in Lebanon until the nineteenth century. In 1921, the villagers of Jabel Druze in Syria received "independence under the French Mandate." Although they were still subordinate to the French authorities, their region was independent from the rest of the country. Despite the failure of the Druze Revolt against the French from 1925 to 1927, they enjoyed certain autonomy until 1944, when Jabel Druze was integrated into independent Syria.

The Druze never gained national independence because that was not their goal. Throughout their history, they took a realistic approach to life. Although they were determined to protect their rights, they never developed a distinct national movement because they knew they would not be strong enough to confront other national movements. At the same time, they did not want to create a buffer between themselves and their Arab neighbors. After all, ethnically they are Arabs. But, like their Arab brethren, protecting their lands has become a sacred value, second only to protecting the family and its honor.

DRUZE RELIGION

MOSTLY, THE DRUZE ARE A deeply religious people. Religion plays a dominant role in both their private and communal life. The Druze religion is considerably secretive, not just to us "heathens," but also within the Druze community itself. The Druze's holy scriptures are not supposed to be printed, and only a limited group of qualified experts are allowed to handwrite copies of the scriptures.

Although the Druze pride themselves for being a socially cohesive community, they are divided between those who are entitled to the intimate details of the religion, and those who settle for "less" and must remain content with closer ties to this earthly world. The *Uqqal* (the wise) are familiar with the religious teachings, whereas the *Juhal* (the ignorant) are not initiated in the Druze doctrine. When young Druze reach the age of fifteen, they are offered a chance to choose whether they wish to enter through the gates of religious wisdom or remain outside to lead a "business as usual" kind of life.

The Juhal who want to make the jump to becoming "Uqqal" must engage in a long and hard indoctrinating process reminiscent of the demanding conversion procedure in Judaism. They need to study and regularly visit the *Hilwa*, the Druze prayer house. Only those who demonstrate piety and devotion and have withstood the long process of candidacy are initiated into the teachings of the Druze faith.

Women are allowed initiation in the Druze doctrine. In

fact, the Druze tradition considers women more spiritually prepared than men are to enter such circles, because women are considered less likely to be exposed to deviant or immoral practices such as murder and adultery.

To show that they are Druze, men shave their heads, grow a moustache (though not necessarily a beard), put on a white turban, and wear a traditional black gown. Girls will put on a headscarf called *naqab* and a long dress, very much like that of Muslim and Jewish orthodox women. The most pious among the women hide all their hair under a separate covering, the *iraqiyah,* which is fastened around the head under a white scarf. For the sake of modesty, women should not be photographed, nor should they drive, which, according to the clergy, keeps them safe and close to home.

Though most Druze know more than the basic tenets of their religion, such knowledge should be kept from outsiders. Their intention is not to keep all religious wealth to themselves, but to protect the community. As a people that have suffered generations of persecution at the hands of their Muslim and Christian neighbors, they developed the trait of keeping their secrets away from inquisitive, provocative eyes. Their tactics have involved a low-key approach—to let sleeping dogs lie, as long as the dogs don't bite them. Whenever the Druze have been attacked, they reacted vigorously, hitting back hard, thus acquiring their reputation as fearless warriors. This is why their service in the Israel Defense Forces—unlike the Arab population, which is exempt from military service—is part of a generations-long tradition; always on the alert, always ready to defend themselves, no matter what.

The secrecy surrounding Druze religion has occasionally been counterproductive, having the effect of arousing curiosity—and fear—rather than defending the faith. Throughout history, Druze have faced campaigns of defamation, with religious rivals often describing the Druze in diabolical terms.

Despite their secretiveness, the Druze are so confident in their religion that, even when their holy scriptures have fallen into alien hands, they were not really concerned. In their book *The Druze* (2001), Druze writers Samih Natour and Akram Hasson recount a story about the "immunity" of their scriptures in the face of enemies. In the 1830s, the Druze residents of the Horan region in Syria revolted against the invading Egyptian army. Egyptian soldiers captured Druze holy scriptures in a Horan village and handed them over to curious French "experts" on Druze theology. "We have cracked the secrets of the Druze religion," boasted the French experts. "Never mind," ridiculed Druze religious leaders; "they will not understand them anyway. They *think* they will, but they won't, because the Scriptures are written in a secret code."

From what we *do* know about the moral basics of Druze religion, there are no revolutionary concepts to be revealed, as compared to its predecessors, Judaism, Christianity, and Islam. They adopted similar principles, such as love of truth, communal solidarity, renouncing all other religions, avoiding the demon and all wrongdoers, accepting the unity of God, and submitting to the will of God. So where is the difference, at least as Druze see it? Although the Druze recognize all three monotheistic religions, they believe that rituals and ceremonies have caused Jews, Christians, and Muslims to turn aside from "pure faith."

The Druze do not regard themselves to be Muslims, although they split from Islam. Unlike the Muslims, the Druze have eliminated all elements of ritual and ceremony; there is no fixed daily liturgy, no defined holy days, no fasting during the month of Ramadan, and no pilgrimage obligations. The Druze practice their spiritual reckoning with God at all times and consequently have no need for special days of fasting or atonement. Moreover, unlike Islam, which allows a man as many as four wives, Druze religion strictly bans polygamy. On the other hand, the Druze adopted the Islamic ban on eating pork, drinking alcohol, and smoking. The first two are widely observed, but smoking ... well, that's a habit that even the fear of God cannot uproot.

One more aspect of Druze religion is so different from the other main religions that it gets its own chapter.

REINCARNATION

FOR THREE LONG DAYS AND nights the rescue team dug underneath the wreckage, pulling out bodies and remains of bodies, hoping to save but losing hope. Three days earlier, on November 11, 1982, the entire complex of the military government command in the Biblical town of Tyre in south Lebanon collapsed in a giant blast. Eventually they counted seventy-five bodies of young soldiers, border police, and General Security Service agents. One of the dead was Fuad Sa'ad, twenty-three, a soldier from the Druze village of Beit Jann in Upper Galilee.

Now, twenty-three years after his death, he is sitting next to us on the terrace of his family home in Beit Jann, very much alive. His eyes swallow the green mountains surrounding the village; his body drinks the fresh mountain air; and he radiates an air of contentment. Life has been good to him. Fuad Izzi of 2005, a soldier serving in Gaza, and Fuad Sa'ad who was killed in Tyre are one and the same. This is the belief of his family, the parents of "the previous" Fuad, and the entire community. The two Fuads simply switched bodies, but the soul and the spirit are the same.

* * *

Belief in reincarnation is one of the pillars of Druze religion and heritage, similar to the five pillars of Islam. The Druze believe that the Bible, as well as the Qur'an, carry the message of reincarnation, but only *they* have interpreted it correctly. The Druze believe that the soul reincarnates from one person to another, from a man to a man, a woman to a woman, from a Druze to a Druze. The body is merely a dress. When you die, you simply change dresses. Thus, one of the Arabic words for reincarnation is *takkamus,* which originates from the word *kamis,* or shirt.

The Druze do not claim exclusiveness to reincarnation but say that they experience it in a stronger manner because it is so dominant in their creed. Druze children, sometimes as young as three years old, can actually speak about and reconstruct their past lives. This trait is referred to as *nutuk,* or speech.

Fuad Izzi was three years old when he went down the street, hand-in-hand with his mother, and made his first "speech." To this day he remembers how he suddenly approached a woman, pointed a finger at her, and said, "Toof."

"Neither Mother nor the woman understood what I meant. For a moment they thought I meant toffee, the candy, but the woman had no toffee. It turned out that the woman's name was Itaf, and then I began citing the names of all members of the family, including Fuad, her son who was killed in Tyre.

"I remember everything that had happened to her son Fuad, because I *am* Fuad, the reincarnated version of the dead soldier."

He tells the story as if he were *really* there, as though it had *really* happened to him personally. "It was a Thursday. I was about to go home for the weekend, but my friends insisted that, before I go, I should sit down and have coffee with them. Suddenly there was a huge explosion, the whole building collapsed, and I lost consciousness. The next thing I remember is someone slapping my face, trying to wake me up. I wanted to respond, but I couldn't. Eventually I died in the hospital.

"As a child, I recognized all the members of the family. When I went to the kindergarten I recognized my uncle from my previous life, I hugged him warmly, and I said, 'Uncle Jamal!'"

Thus, Druze life repeats itself in an endless cycle. Death is less frightening, and bereavement is less painful. "Death is also hard for us—losing friends and relatives," said Fuad. "But, at a certain stage you feel relieved to know that maybe, maybe, you'll meet the dead again, knowing that he'll be born to other people.

"God willing, the dead will remember who he was in the prior life and will come to see his friends and get to know his parents. His soul will remain for eternity."

Fuad Izzi is not eccentric. Talk to people in all twenty-one Druze villages, and you will hear similar stories, sometimes even more amazing. Usually, they are reluctant to share their stories with outsiders, first, because it is part of the religious no-entry zone, and second, because they are well aware of the suspicious distrust when rational Jews make up the audience. The story of Lutfi Nasser a-Din was contributed to us by his father, and by Wissam, his reincarnated embodiment.

* * *

It was the last day of Lutfi's military service. The previous evening, he had called his father, Amal. "That's it," said Lutfi, "I am coming home tomorrow." The year was 1969. Lutfi was stationed in the Arava desert in the south, patrolling the border with Jordan. It was a violent border, with hot pursuits after Palestinian fighters on terrorist missions crossing the fields into Israel.

Lutfi was in a jolly mood. He would soon return home, this

time for good. In the morning he would go the army discharge unit. "Let me talk to my daughter," he asked his father. "Your daughter?" laughed Amal, "she is only forty-days old!!"

"Never mind," said Lutfi, "punch her, make her laugh, make her cry, I want to hear her voice."

It was the last time his father and baby-daughter heard his voice. The next morning, Lutfi was just about to mount his jeep to go up north when word came in that a number of suspects had been spotted crossing the lines into Israel. Lutfi's friends in the unit rushed to their vehicles, ready to go on the all-too-familiar terrorist chase. Lutfi joined the boys. "Get the hell out of here," barked David Maimon, Lutfi's commander, "they are waiting for you at the discharge unit!" Nevertheless, Lutfi insisted and joined the other soldiers.

"Lutfi was standing on a cliff above a wadi." Father Amal reconstructs the day's events as if they have just happened. "He didn't see the terrorists in the wadi, but they saw him, and fired directly at him. Lutfi managed to return fire, killed three of them, but a few minutes later, he was dead, too."

At the time, Amal Nasser a-Din was a senior member of the Histadrut labor union. A couple of hours after his son was gunned down, Amal was on his way from the village of Daliat al-Carmel to a meeting in Tel-Aviv. "Halfway between Dalia and Tel-Aviv, my body was overwhelmed with total weakness. I just couldn't go on driving. I turned around and went back home.

"A few hours later, I received a phone call from a senior officer; he wanted to see me at his Haifa office.

"As soon as I entered his office, I understood: Something terrible has happened. Zvi, I asked him, what happened? Which one of my brothers?

"He burst out crying and said, 'None of your brothers. It is your son, Lutfi.'

"I felt as if I was struck by a million-ton rock. 'My son? Didn't he call yesterday that he was on his way to the discharge unit? How come?'"

Thirty-seven years later Amal is still convinced that his dead son returned to life.

The strictly religious Druze, the true believers, keep the intimate details of reincarnation away from the public eye. The family of Fuad Sa'ad, who was killed in Tyre, refused to see us. So did many others with similar stories. It is one thing to circulate such stories among the community, but it is not customary to discuss them in public. Amal's willingness to discuss the reincarnation of his son was exceptional.

"Had it not been for father Amal, I would not have spoken to you," said Wissam Ibrahim, thirty-six, as we sat in his cozy living room (the *diwan*), surrounded by his biological parents, his daughter Rima, his wife, a brother, and a sister.

Wissam is absolutely convinced that he is the incarnated body of Lutfi, Amal's son who fell in the shootout with the terrorists back in 1969. Amal is not Wissam's *real* father, but Wissam treats him as such.

"At the time, Lutfi's death meant nothing to me, beyond the natural sorrow over the loss of a young life and the fact that Amal was a well-known personality in the Druze community," recalled Wissam's father, Zaki Ibrahim. The Ibrahim family lives in the Galilee village of Sajour, about an hour's drive north of Daliat al-Carmel, Amal's village. Zaki did not attend Lutfi's funeral, although it had turned into a communal event, with some thirty thousand Druze following the coffin. He did not really know the family of the fallen soldier. He was busy, in fact, with family festivities over the birth of his son Wissam, on the very day that Lutfi was killed.

Only years later did he realize that Wissam and Lutfi were one and the same. "Wissam was not an easy child," recalled Zaki. "He was mischievous, hyperactive, never content, often crying. Whenever he was cross with us, he used to shout at us, 'You are not my parents! Take me to my parents!'

"We used to ignore him; we thought he picked something from friends and tried to manipulate us. We thought these were just childhood hallucinations."

Every now and then, the child used to pack some clothes in a parcel and run away, to the mountain. Moreover, there was another strange aspect of his behavior. Young Wissam could not stand the sight of his uncle Nazem, his father's brother. Whenever Nazem entered the room, Wissam ran away. He would never talk to him. No one knew why.

"When Nazem used to come here, I used to cry that I didn't like him I used to leave the room until he left the house. They thought I was weird, to say the least." Only much later, he says now, did he resolve the mystery of his behavior.

Then, something happened that convinced the family that the child knew what he was talking about. A group of the electric company workers were busy linking the house to the national power system. One of the workers was Amin Hassoon from Daliat al-Carmel. Four-year-old Wissam just wouldn't take his eyes off Amin. Every time the team began working, Wissam left the house, clinging to Amin, attracted to him by some magic force, refusing to leave the work site. Amin often lost patience with the child, concerned that he might be hurt. "Child, go away," he commanded, but Wissam would not listen.

One day, Amin grabbed Wissam by the hand, and took him home. Wissam cried, opening a crack to his secret: "He was my friend before I was killed, why is he cross with me?" Although Wissam's parents did not believe the story, Amin, the electric company worker, suspected something. He had been a close friend of Lutfi Nasser a-Din.

A few days later he returned to the village with a photo album in hand and showed it to young Wissam. "I looked at the pictures and I identified each and every one of them. This is Lutfi; this is father Amal; these are my friends. It was *my* family album."

The parents were stunned. They drove with the child to Daliat al-Carmel. As they reached the village center, Wissam wanted out of the car. "Don't ask anyone," he ordered his parents, "I will show you where I used to live." He led his parents to the Nasser a-Din residence, pointed at Amal and said, "This is my father."

* * *

"I remember everything as if it happened yesterday," recalled Amal. "As soon as I saw him I knew he was my son. We looked at each other, we almost cried, but we didn't."

Wissam then began walking around the house, identified his room, he went out to the yard, took a good look around, and asked, "There used to be mulberry tree here, why did you cut it down?" He then pointed in another direction: "And that's where the cowshed stood."

Amal pulled out two pistols. "That one is mine," said Wissam, pointing at the pistol that had belonged to Lutfi.

A young man entered the house. "This is my best friend Fuad," said Wissam. "We bought a lottery ticket together."

No one needed further proof. The lottery ticket still existed; it was still there. He then met Lutfi's widow and their daughter. The two sat quietly and didn't say a word. Four-year-old

Wissam approached them with confidence, kissed each one of them on their forehead, held the girl's hand, and ordered her mother, acting as if he were her deceased husband: "I will play with the child while you prepare dinner."

The mystery of Wissam's dislike for his uncle Nazem was also resolved. It turned out that Nazem and Lutfi attended the same officers' training course. Lutfi was apparently envious of Nazem who excelled in the course. Relations between the two deteriorated. The former friends turned into rivals. Lutfi would not forgive even in his reincarnated soul.

Thirty-seven years later, we sat at the Ibrahim residence, discussing the winding family history. Lutfi, Amal's son, was there, too. A picture of Lutfi was hanging on the wall, a young, handsome boy in uniform, carrying a gun and smiling, as if he had always been there with his new family.

Wissam seemed happy with the opportunity to tell the story. Now, that he had his "father's" authorization, he felt at ease unfolding the details before strangers. His father Zaki recalled how Wissam had changed radically after the meeting with Lutfi's parents. He was no longer the fidgety child, he stopped yelling at his parents, and he did not run away from home. Instead, his parents took him often to meet his other family at Daliat al-Carmel. Amal, in the meantime, had became a Member of the Knesset on the Likud list and often came to visit his "son."

Zaki Ibrahim and his wife Jamila are not envious that their son shared his love with another pair of parents. "I was concerned only that he would be split between us, but he is not."

"I love both my parents, I love them equally," said Wissam.

Wissam married at twenty-two and now has five children. His oldest daughter is called Rima, like the daughter of Lutfi.

* * *

The Druze believe that death is predestined and that there is nothing one can do to avoid it. Taking this belief a step further implies that, as soon as Wissam was conceived, Lutfi's days were numbered. By the time Wissam was born, Lutfi was destined to die. Jamila's pregnancy was in fact Lutfi's death sentence.

"Had I known, I would not have brought Wissam to the world," smiled Zaki Ibrahim, as if he was joking, but he wasn't. He meant it. "I was never religious, I certainly did not believe in God in the religious sense of the word. But after Wissam's revelation I have no doubt that there is some outside force which dictates our lives."

The conversation is held in Hebrew, mixed every now and then with a sentence in Arabic. Young Rima sits on the sofa next to us, about nine years old with long, beautiful hair and shining eyes. She listens attentively as if she understands, although she does not. But then again, she's heard the story repeatedly. By now it has become part of the family's heritage. When Amal comes to visit she calls him grandpa.

"I am glad it happened to me," said Wissam. "It should have made the grief of Amal Nasser a-Din's family easier."

"It has not," Amal told us. "Of course I am happy that my son has found a new, good family, but my pain has not been relieved. I still mourn my child."

Even Israeli Jews, who are quite familiar with Druze customs find it hard to cope with the fact that Druze belief in reincarnation is not just superstition rather than a way of life. However, one cannot understand the Druze community without grasping the depth of that belief. The belief is shared by the young and the old, men and women, the most educated to the least.

Jewish mysticism, too, believes that the soul of a dead person finds shelter in a new body, but it is difficult, even for a Jewish believer, to grasp the belief in fore-life and afterlife as an integral part of everyday life. We came a step closer to understanding this after we met with Professor Fadel Mansour.

Just a few minutes drive from Haifa University on Mt. Carmel, we find ourselves in the heart of "Druzeland." Issfiya and Daliat al-Carmel are two Druze villages strategically located on top of the mountain, its residents spoiled by vistas of carpets of pine trees, the magnificent Gulf of Haifa and, further north, the ancient town of Acre.

The Druze who settled on Mt. Carmel came from Mt. Lebanon and the Halab region in Syria. They were fleeing the continuous blood feuds within their own community as well as with their Christian and Muslim neighbors. The hills of Mt. Carmel would be calmer, or so they had hoped. The Druze who settled in Palestine built their villages on top of the mountains, just as they had done in Lebanon and Syria, making it easier to defend themselves against tribal rivals, gaining the beautiful landscapes as a bonus.

"In our family, we count ten generations back, so we must have been here for 350 years," said Professor Fadel Mansur, our host in Issfiya.

In the years since the establishment of the State of Israel, Issfiya and neighboring Daliat al-Carmel have turned from communal hideouts into tourist attractions. Every weekend, the streets that cut through those two villages are crammed with Israeli Jews from the city, seeking authentic Druze folklore, fresh mountain air, delicious meals, and an outpouring of the legendary Druze hospitality.

Few people in Israel, and perhaps in the entire region, can match Druze friendliness and openness. Anyone entering a

Dr. Ruth visits the Mansour family in Issfiya. Mother Najwa, Dr. Ruth, daughter Yarin, 12, son Ayal, 17 and father Ghassan. Ayal's t-shirt says "Respect."

Druze home—or, for that matter a Druze shop, restaurant, or you name it—is greeted as if one's visit is the best thing that had ever happened to the hosts. Even better, the smiles are never artificial. A visitor feels *truly* welcome and the best thing that has happened to the host that day.

We took a turn to the right from the road cutting through Issfiya—jammed with scores of cars of shopping-starved and food-hungry Israelis—and drove up the driveway of the Mansour housing complex that included five brothers and five houses, an actual manifestation of the Druze family desire to stick together. Unlike life in America, a Druze does not need to catch a plane to visit a brother during the holidays. Unlike the Jews in Israel, one does not need to hit the highway. The Druze will usually meet their kin within walking distance from home.

Professor Fadel Mansour opens the door of his spacious

house, and my crew and I are immediately struck by three features: a colorful, round head cover, a generous, friendly smile, and an impressive, huge, curly moustache.

Mansour is a religious person. The shaved head and his beard, the head cover and the moustache, are all external features of an observant Druze. The big smile and shining eyes are all his. Meet Mansour and you will understand the Druze much better. At the age of sixty, his hands are still busy with scientific research, yet he doesn't turn down invitations to lecture on the Druze community. He jumps from a gathering of Arab women to a meeting of soldiers, recounting the history of the community, surprised to discover time and again how little everyone knows about his people, although he admits, "You will be surprised how little the Druze know about themselves."

Mansour is a senior researcher at the department of entomology of the prestigious Neve Ya'ar Research Center of the Agricultural Research Organization, better known as the Volcani Institute. He is an expert on biological control of spider mites, host plant resistance to mites, and biologically produced acaracides.

Mansour has recently come up with a discovery that could revolutionize our eating habits. In his search for mite-resistant plants, he found an east-Asian plant that scares away all mites and can be used to store fruits and other foods for long periods without the danger of being penetrated by mites and, most important, eliminating the need to use pesticides in their growth.

We mention all this to make the point that Mansour is not a shaman but a rational person who requires proof to establish facts. He is a scientist. Primarily, however, Mansour is a community leader. Mansour has the intellect of a professor, the charm of an actor, the eloquence of a clergyman. Given that the Druze community lacks effective leaders, it's too bad he hasn't made it to the Knesset or even to a ministerial position. It is therefore particularly enlightening to hear a down-to-earth scientist like Mansour refer to reincarnation not only in religious and metaphysical terms, but also in purely scientific terminology.

Mansour's starting point is philosophical. He explains that, in a way, reincarnation is the Druze answer to the classic dilemma of Ecclesiastes "that there be just *men*, unto whom it happeneth according to the work of the wicked; again, there be wicked *men*, to whom it happeneth according to the work of the righteous." Punishment is either to pay for past evil or because one is evil now. In other words, punishment or reward for one's deeds does not necessarily occur immediately in one's present life, but can come later in a future life. Reward and punishment may not come until after several incarnations, depending on the spirit's ability to improve itself from one life to the next. Once we accept the premise that our moral responsibility does not end when we pass away, we can take a step further in the walk of afterlife and deal with reincarnation using Mansour's scientific arguments.

Mansour explains that, after death, the soul moves to another body in a sort of unknown divine energy, which a human being cannot grasp. "But the fact that we cannot identify that energy does not mean that it doesn't exist. People think that they know everything, but actually they know nothing."

Very well; granted, we know very little, and this is why we do not recognize this energy. Further, by the same logic, our lack of knowledge is no proof that the energy does exist. At best, we should give the energy of reincarnation the benefit of doubt; it may exist, and yet it may not exist. Fifty-fifty. But Mansour answers philosophically that the very argument over its existence proves that it exists.

Of course I had some follow-up questions for Mansour. If indeed, one soul transforms into the other, how come world population grows? Where do all those "new" souls come from? In the year 2000, the world had 6.1 billion inhabitants according to United Nations figures. For the last fifty years, world population multiplied more rapidly than ever before.

This is a question Mansour faces repeatedly from skeptics like us. His smile suddenly appears mocking, almost haughty. "How do we know that this is the size of world population?" he asks. "These are only estimates. Look, while the population in Egypt and other countries in Africa is growing, population in Europe and China decreases." According to Druze belief, the total doesn't change—7.25 billion people in the entire world, with souls wondering from a dead person to a new life.

Naturally, Gil and I had more questions, like: Why has world population been fixed on that figure exactly? And whatever happened to the Biblical story of creation and Adam and Eve? Certainly, Mansour would have had all the answers at hand, but we felt that we should leave it at that, and be content with knowing that perhaps the Druze are right, and God will indeed give us another chance.

Some Druze object to implantation of live organs from non-Druze or, worse yet, from animals, as if the Druze recipient is thus made impure.

"Nonsense," ruled Mansour. "The body is not important; the body is just a tool that serves the soul, and that's why you can receive the heart of a Jew or even a pig."

Fuad Izzi of Beit Jann told us that the parents of the dead Fuad treat him as their son. "Had I fallen in love with the daughter of the previous Fuad, I don't think I could marry her, because actually she is *my* daughter.

"I know of a girl in the village of Peki'in who was just about to be married, when she began to tell stories, indicating that in the previous life she was the mother of her bridegroom. The wedding was cancelled."

"This, too, is nonsense," said Mansour, for the same reason: The body is only a tool, a transit station.

Belief in reincarnation makes bereavement easier. "A Druze mother will find the loss of her son easier to accept than a Jewish mother, not only because she knows that her son now lives in another body, but also because she believes that the moment of death is predestined and that there was nothing that could have prevented it. Theoretically, a son can get married on the same day that his father dies."

As a result, mourning customs are different. Because the body is valueless after death, the family usually refrains from visiting the grave after burial. There are no official days of mourning. The one exception is mourning over soldiers who have fallen in battle. The military graveyard in Issfiya is located across the street from the Mansour housing complex. It is well-kept, and bereaved families visit the graves of their children on the official Remembrance Day.

"I object," says Mansour. "Those visits open up wounds. I know the intention is good, but this is an alien and even dangerous custom. Do we have to accept all Jewish customs, even their mourning customs?"

Mansour is concerned that this is yet another factor of assimilation that the Druze are trying so hard to avert.

* * *

While the Druze are certainly to be admired for their many fine qualities like extreme hospitality and courage in fighting, they are still human beings with earthly faults. Take gossip, for example. Talk to a Druze about another Druze, and you are likely to hear libel. No one is more critical of the Druze community than the Druze themselves. As the old Jewish saying goes, there is no joy like malicious joy. Perhaps they learned it from the Jews.

Talk to a Druze about Druze politicians, and your ears are likely to burn. Talk to a Druze about the community as a whole, however, and you will hear only praise. The Druze in Israel—a minority within the Arab minority within the Israeli society—are a very proud group of people. "The Druze may bow their heads in submission up to a certain point, but when they are fed up with suffering, they burst out like crazy," said Professor Fadel Mansour.

THE DRUZE IN ISRAEL

ALI BIRANI WAS TWELVE YEARS OLD WHEN he first saw that strange-looking creature who spoke a language he did not understand, did not wear any head cover, and wore those funny, uncomfortable garments, virtually glued to his body and totally different from the loose, airy Druze garments. The stranger was the Jewish doctor from a neighboring kibbutz who came to the village of Daliat al-Carmel once a week to treat his Druze patients.

Soon, one Jewish visitor followed another, and Ali learned that the "Yahud" (Arabic for "Jews") were often considered better friends than the villagers' Christian and Muslim neighbors. The year was 1948, the days of war preceding the establishment of the State of Israel. The Druze were caught in the crossfire between the Jews and the Palestinians. At times, the Palestinians attacked Druze villages, whose citizens had cooperated with the Jews. The doctor's visits were a manifestation of the strengthening ties between the Jewish *Yishuv* (the pre-state political organization of the Jews in Palestine) and the small Druze community of some ten thousand inhabitants.

Now few Druze can boast of such a wide network of personal contacts with influential Israeli Jews as Ali Birani, at seventy, can. After years of intense communal activities and having held numerous public offices, his contacts can be found throughout all levels of Israeli society. He was a former advisor to the minister of tourism and was among those who established the military government in the occupied territories following the 1967 Six-Day War. Now retired, he is president of the Israeli Inter-Religious and International Federation for World Peace-Israel. He often opens his home to guests from all walks of life, thus serving as a de facto liaison between the Druze and other communities. In a way, he is the unofficial foreign minister of the Druze community. Birani's close ties with his Jewish compatriots are not just a partnership of convenience; it is a way of life. Any Jew who knows Birani will boast that Ali is a "personal friend" or, better yet, "a member of the family." Ali personifies the current Jewish–Druze partnership.

Druze researcher Dr. Shimon Avivi discovered that back in the twelfth century a Jewish traveler, Binyamin Mitudela, wrote that the Druze liked the Jews and preferred to trade with them. Historian Yitzhak Ben-Zvi (later Israel's second president), identified fourteen Jewish villages among the Druze in Mt. Lebanon. Small Jewish communities in Palestine preferred to live within Druze villages, such as Peki'in in upper Galilee, rather than near Muslim or Christian communities. These contacts paved the way for the warm relations with the Jews during the time of the Yishuv, the Zionist entity in Palestine. It was an alliance of convenience between two ethnic groups that were each a minority within Palestine, inhabited mostly by Arabs at the time.

It was not love at first sight. During the 1929 anti-Zionist riots, Palestinian leaders tried to recruit veterans of the Druze revolt against the French government in Syria, whose members had fled to Transjordan. British authorities, who were in charge in both Palestine and Transjordan, prevented the plot. The Druze leadership in Palestine faced a dilemma: Should it join the anti-Zionist struggle? Should it remain neutral? Should it side with the Jews?

It was not an easy choice for such a small minority. Each alternative presented dangers, because each could alienate one or both parties in the conflict. A relatively minor incident in 1930 brought the two communities closer together. A Druze robber murdered a Palestinian police officer near the Galilee village of Rami. The local police—mostly Palestinian—staged a punitive raid against the nearby village of Mughar. To put an end to what they perceived as the persecution of the Druze, the local Druze leaders asked for the help of the Zionist leadership in reaching the national police command. As a result, senior Jewish Agency officials went to Transjordan and met with Druze notables. Thus was born the political dialogue that led to the strongest bonds between the Jews and any Arab group in the Middle East.

Although some Druze volunteers and mercenaries participated in the Arab Revolt of 1936 to 1939, others, predominantly in the Druze villages on Mt. Carmel, nurtured their ties with the Jews. As a result, at one point, Palestinians villagers in Umm a-Zinat attacked the nearby Druze villages of Daliat al-Carmel and Issfiya. When the attackers passed the Birani residence, they spotted what seemed to be a big Star of David depicted at the entrance to the house, and were prepared to kill its Jewish inhabitants. The owner of the house was Ali's father Na'im, a devout Druze. It was not the Star of David but what the Druze call "Solomon's Seal," a five-edged red-green-yellow-blue and white star, symbolizing principles of the religion such as truth, courage, soul, patience, and peace. The Palestinian gang detained Na'im Birani and sentenced him to death, but he was eventually released in exchange for a few horses.

Relations between the Druze and the Arabs soured, while relations between the Druze and Jews grew stronger, further strengthened when many Druze were sent on intelligence missions. At one point, both Jewish and Druze leaders entertained the idea that the Druze in Palestine would resettle on Jabel Druze (Mt. Druze) in Syria, and the Jews would purchase their lands on Mt. Carmel. The initiative was foiled, though, with the outbreak of World War II.

The fact that the Druze had no national aspirations helped strengthen their ties with the Jews. The Birani family was one of the first to declare openly that, whatever the outcome of the Jewish–Palestinian conflict, they would stick with the Jews. Na'im Birani and his brother Hussein made a living supplying food to the besieged Jewish settlements of Beit Oren and Ya'arot Ha'Carmel.

Ali still lives in the house of his father and grandfather in the village of Daliat al-Carmel, one of twenty-one villages and one town (Shefaramer) on Mt. Carmel and in the Galilee in the northern part of the country. Some sixteen thousand Druze live in four villages on the Golan Heights. Israel conquered the Golan in the Six-Day War of 1967, and eventually annexed it to become an integral part of the country. However, most of the Druze residents of the Golan identify themselves as Syrians, in sharp contrast with the strong Israeli identity of their brethren in the Galilee and the Carmel. (We will discuss this situation later at length.)

A visit to the Birani residence is never just a visit. It is always accompanied by a rich and generous meal, the best of the Druze kitchen. The variety of food usually includes mutton, rice, rich and spicy salads, yogurt, humus, and freshly baked pitas, everything cooked and accompanied by olive oil. When the Druze open their doors to guests, they also open their tables, loaded with the best of Druze cuisine. It is not just a matter of politeness; it is a way of life. At social gatherings, the women of the Birani house work energetically from the early

Baking pita breads.

hours of the day, to make sure that no one will leave hungry. No one ever does. Ali Birani:

"I was in the sixth grade when I had a teacher from Nablus who used to say that the Jews are sons of the Devil. I told him he was talking nonsense. 'I know the Jews, and they are not as you describe them.' The teacher was disappointed in me. He called me *Sahyouni,* a Zionist. Twenty years later, after the Six-Day War, I met him in Nablus. This time he told me how much he regretted that the Palestinians had not made peace with the Jews a long time ago."

Even Sheikh Amin Tarif, who later became a champion of that alliance, was at first hesitant and advocated neutrality in the Jewish–Palestinian conflict, adopting a policy of waiting to see who would have the upper hand in that conflict. However, by April 1948, with the defeat of the expeditionary force from

Syria in one battle and the defeat of a pro-Palestinian Druze battalion in yet another battle, Druze leaders understood that they were better off siding with the Jews.

During the early stages of the 1948 war, the Druze in Jabel Druze in Syria and the Shouf Mountains in Lebanon sent a battalion of volunteers to Palestine to help "the brethren in Palestine in case the Jews might do them harm." The battalion was deployed near the village of Shefaramer, just north of Haifa. It so happened that the Druze battalion was thrown into the battle zone, just as the Arabs were suffering strategic defeats. One such defeat was the failure of the Syrian expeditionary force led by Kaukji to take over kibbutz Mishmar Ha'emek east of Haifa.

Kaukji was desperate. On April 11, 1948, he sent a cable to the commander of the Druze battalion in Shefaramer: "I am pleading with you, children of the Druze. I am in trouble, if you don't come to my rescue, I will plea to God."

The Druze battalion tried to break the Jewish resistance around Haifa, by attacking kibbutz Ramat Yohanan, at the foot of the Carmel Mountain. It was a cruel and bloody battle. The Druze stormed the kibbutz, wave after wave, unable to conquer the kibbutz, with both sides suffering heavy losses. One of the Jewish casualties was Zorik Dayan, the brother of Moshe Dayan, Israel's legendary fighter who later became chief of staff, minister of defense, and minister of foreign affairs.

As the battle raged, the Haganah commanders urged the local Druze leaders to intervene. They agreed, met with the commanders of the Druze battalion, and asked them to stop the fighting, convincing them that the Druze were facing no danger from the Jews. A truce was signed. The Druze battalion returned home, with some of its fighters staying in Palestine and even joining the Jews. One of the Druze commanders, Ismayil Kabalan, later joined the IDF and became a senior Israeli army officer. Consequently, Haganah commanders and Druze leaders signed a nonaggression pact. Those were the last of hostilities between Druze and Jews and the beginning of the Druze–Jewish alliance.

By April 1948, a month before the establishment of the Jewish state, young Druze joined the Haganah, the Jewish defense organization that preceded the formation of the state of Israel. During Israel's War of Independence it was only natural for the Druze community to side with the Jews. They did not flee like the Palestinians, but remained in their villages.

In the early days of the state, an experts' committee recommended that the government treat the minorities according to their socioeconomic levels, not by their communal or political affiliation. The working hypothesis was that those who were better off were less likely to engage in anti-Israeli activities. This applied to the Druze as well. Although the committee was appointed by Premier David Ben-Gurion, he nevertheless rejected its recommendations. They contradicted the traditional Zionist policy of trying to establish an alliance of minorities in the Middle East and forcing a wedge between the Druze and the Muslims living in the country.

Despite the rejection of those recommendations, the official policy toward the Druze in the early days of the state was one of "respect and suspect."

Druze loyalty to their own community supersedes all other allegiances. This is why at first the General Security Service suspected more than respected them. The heads of the GSS remembered the battle of Ramat Yohanan in which the Druze sided with the forces that invaded from Syria, and they were concerned that, given the right circumstances, the Druze might

Druze members of Israeli armed forces with film crew.

once again join Israel's enemies. However, Ben-Gurion, who had the final word on virtually *everything,* gave the green light for the full integration of the Druze community. By 1956, the Druze leadership had accepted compulsory military service, from which other Arab citizens of Israel are exempt. It was hoped that, if young Druze served in the army alongside the Jews, they would receive rights equal to those of the Jews. This hope has yet to materialize.

After Shimon Avivi retired from the prestigious Mossad (the Israeli intelligence service) and its pursuit of enemies of the state, he switched to the academic quest of pursuing the Druze story. The Yad Ben-Zvi research institute in Jerusalem plans to publish his book based on his Ph.D dissertation: "The Druze in Israel: the Policy of the Government toward the Druze Minority,

'48–'67." It will be the deepest and most thorough study ever written of the Jewish state's treatment of its Druze minority—a story that, so far, has been told only in bits and pieces.

Unfortunately, the story is cut—somewhat arbitrarily—at that crucial crossroads of 1967, when Israel within a six-day period, went from being a state under a ghetto-like siege to becoming the strongest regional power. The primary reason for the cut-off was quite mundane: Documents of the National Archive dated later than 1967 are classified. Thus, Avivi, had he desired to pursue his studies beyond that watershed period would be missing an invaluable research tool.

Further, he decided to stop at that year for another, quite substantial reason: The status of the Druze, like all Israelis, changed radically in 1967. They, too, were transformed over those same six days from a tolerated, insignificant minority into an important element in the country's defense establishment. Until a year before the Six-Day War, most Druze villages were under military government rule, like all Arab villages. Yet now they were recruited en masse to staff the military government apparatus, which controlled the territories of occupied Syria, Jordan, and Egypt. They possessed an asset that most Israelis were missing—Arabic, their mother tongue. They had become full partners with the Jews—or *almost* full partners. On paper, they were partners, but in practice the Druze population in Israel suffers a certain measure of discrimination even today.

In 1967, Israel's entire Arab population was transformed from a humiliated minority, still suffering the consequences of the 1948 defeat, into a proud Israeli community. When Israel's Palestinians compared their situation to that of their brethren in the occupied territories, they realized that they had gotten the better deal. They were better off economically, socially, and politically. Paradoxically, the Palestinians in Israel felt freer in the Jewish state than they did in any of the neighboring Arab countries.

Moreover, what was true for Israel's entire Palestinian population was even truer for the Druze population, whose sons had served in the triumphant Israeli army in the Six-Day War. The fruits were quick to fall. With more and more Druze wage earners serving in the various branches of the security forces, the standard of living improved; Druze villages opened up to small industries, women went out to work, and life was getting better.

By now more than half of the Druze wage earners are employees of the various security branches. Thus, although their level of education is lower than that of their Arab neighbors, their standard of living is higher. Most of the security branches are closed off to the Arab population. Even so, however, the Druze's standard of living lags behind that of the Jews—and sometimes that of the larger minority of Arabs. Druze villages are not as well developed as Jewish settlements; very little was done to create industrial zones close to the Druze villages; unemployment is still quite high; and Druze—like the Christian and Muslim Arabs—face difficulties finding jobs in the civil service.

"There is a constructural problem," said Avivi. "Even when policy makers adopt the right decisions vis-à-vis the Druze population, Jewish civil service bureaucrats often treat them like Arabs, maintaining the old nasty approach of 'respect and suspect.'" Unfortunately, there are just too many examples of discrimination of Druze citizens, which is part of the wider scope of discrimination of all Arab citizens.

The Border Patrol is full of young Druze recruits, but when the Druze reach security checks at Israel's border terminal, they are frequently subjected to the same humiliating security checks that Israel's Arab citizens must endure, a practice often criticized by civil rights groups.

One such unfortunate incident involved the wife of Res. Col. As'ad As'ad, who was about to board an El-Al plane to join her husband serving with the Israeli delegation to the U.N. in New York. Although she possessed a diplomatic passport, she was ordered to step aside from the regular security line for the kind of scrutiny usually "reserved" for Arab passengers.

The highly successful Gush Tefen industrial zone lies in upper Galilee, within several Druze villages. Rather than creating a Druze regional council, however, which would have benefited from taxes paid by the industrial plants, the government created a Jewish regional council, leaving the Druze municipalities aside to beg—and protest. The "Development Region A" government classification—which carries a substantial package of economic benefits—had been given to all Jewish settlements along the border with Lebanon, but Druze border villages did not receive that benefit. The government put an end to that outrageous discrimination only after Druze mayors, led by Knesset Members Selah Tarif (Labor) and As'ad As'ad (Likud), threatened to create a coalition crisis.

Local textile factories, which had employed hundreds of Druze women inside their villages and close to home, were closed down and moved to Jordan because labor there is much cheaper. The only real industry in a Druze village, the Kadamani metal works in the village of Yarka, failed, and there was no one out there to save it.

"There is no intentional policy of discrimination against the Druze," said Avivi, "but the authorities just don't care."

In addition, there is that common popular discrimination, like the case of Druze soldiers, who during their weekend vacations are banned from entering pubs in Haifa because they are suspect as Arabs.

In 1995 the government finally introduced a $300 million, five-year development plan for the Druze villages. This did indeed give a real boost to the Druze villages, but that was the last of it. Since 1999, there is no special money for the Druze local council, and they can barely maintain the investments of the past.

The catch is that the collection of local taxes by Druze municipalities suffers because of *Hamula* (large family clans) politics. Many local politicians fail to sanction tax evaders, not just because they are shy about provoking family members, but also because they know that without the family vote bloc they do not stand a chance to win the local elections. Nevertheless, government financial support of the municipalities is linked to local taxation. In other words, as local taxation diminishes, so does government financial aid. Local authorities lose twice.

"But then Druze mayors cry out against the discrimination of the Druze village of Hurfesh in comparison with the nearby development town of Shlomi," said Avivi. "Only, they forget to mention that tax collection in Shlomi is much higher."

Similarly, Avivi noted that Druze representation in the civil service is much lower than their proportion in the population, and that their educational standards are lower than those of their Arab neighbors. The Arabs, who are exempt from military service, often continue to the institutions of higher learning straight out of high school, whereas young Druze men must first enter a three-year military service. Once they have finished their military service, many get married. At that point they need to support a family, so fewer Druze can afford an additional four years of university studies.

The major exception to discrimination against the Druze has been their full integration into the security establishment. Defense Minister Moshe Arens (1990–1992) was the first to order that all positions be open to the Druze. Today, one Druze serves as major general in the IDF and another as brigadier general, and a Druze officer heads the national Border Guard. A Druze also served as deputy minister of education in the Sharon government.

Contrary to early concerns, the Druze have demonstrated total loyalty to the state throughout the years—despite the occasional trying times. During the Six-Day War, for example, Druze reserve soldiers were not called up to avoid the possibility that Israeli Druze soldiers would have to fight Syrian or Jordanian Druze soldiers. Professor Fadel Mansour of Issfiya, one of our more enlightening hosts during our visit to the Druze, was still a student in 1967. He participated in a demonstration with other students in front of the defense ministry in Tel-Aviv, demanding that they, too, be drafted. On the other hand, during the Lebanon War, when Israel seemed to prefer its Christian allies because of the Lebanese Druze community, a handful of Druze soldiers deserted the IDF and joined their brethren in Lebanon, though they were an insignificant number in comparison to the thousands who had served in the army.

"In fifty-eight years there were very few cases in which Druze have acted against the security of the state," said Avivi, "fewer than Jews."

The Druze and the Second Lebanon War

The second Lebanon War (July and August 2006) strengthened the Jewish–Druze alliance. Mostly, the Druze of the Middle East, whether in Israel or in neighboring Arab countries, did not like the menacing face of Hezbollah leader Sheikh Hassan Nasrallah and feared his rockets. Indeed, several Druze villages, including Peki'in in upper Galilee and Mughar in the lower Galilee, suffered direct hits. A woman and two children were killed in Mughar.

Riad Ali, a journalist, with whom we have held lengthy conversations while working on this book, is a resident of Mughar. In sharp contrast to the pro-Hezbollah trend among Israel's Arab population, he came out strongly against Nasrallah. He wrote an article in *Ma'ariv*, comparing the "Islamic Nation" to an impotent man who finally manages to get a "temporary erection" and deludes himself into thinking that life is still ahead of him. "The Muslim world is engulfed by a Saladin whenever someone succeeds to launch missiles at Israel," wrote Ali. (Saladin was the Muslim warrior who defeated the Crusaders in 1187 and assumed control of Jerusalem.) "Saladin's mission should be redefined, from liberating Jerusalem to liberating the Muslims from those who trade with dreams and disseminate hatred."

Three days later, Ali published an article in another Israeli newspaper, *Ha'aretz*, charging that, "if until the year 2000

Hezbollah could enjoy the benefit of doubt and claim that it was fighting to rid Lebanon of Israeli occupation, today it is obvious to all that it is fighting against the Jews wherever they are."

Riad Ali's comments reflected the general mood among the Druze in the Middle East, who are weary of Hezbollah militancy. Lebanese Druze leader Walid Jumblatt compared Nasrallah to "Adolf Hitler [who] also aroused his people's sense of honor and led Germany into war."

In an interview with the *Chicago Tribune* on August 11, 2006, Jumblatt emerged as a lone voice of dissent amid the clamor of pro-Hezbollah cheerleading that has gripped much of Lebanon and turned Hezbollah leader Hassan Nasrallah into a national hero. Jumblatt is the leader of the 400,000-strong Druze minority in Lebanon and one of the country's most powerful politicians. In an interview at his three-hundred-year-old family castle, he said, "If I were opportunistic I would tell you now, 'Long live Nasrallah.' I am not going to tell you that. I know my position is not popular, in the Arab world or in Lebanon. But I will stick to my position."

In the view of this former-warlord-turned-politician, Hezbollah is fighting not on behalf of Lebanon but as a proxy of Syria and Iran, pursuing an agenda of challenging America that will lead ultimately to Lebanon's ruin. He has no doubt that Hezbollah will eventually win. "But at what price?" he asked. "What is the price?"

Jumblatt said he understands the surge in support for Hezbollah. "Their fighters have done a good job defying and defeating the Israeli army," he says. "But the question we ask is where their allegiance goes: to a Lebanese strong central authority or somewhere else?" Jumblatt was the only political leader who regularly and publicly warned against the consequences of a Hezbollah victory. He believes that such an out-come would bring Lebanon under the tutelage of Iran and Syria once again—just as it was in the 1980s.

"It's a big power play between the Iranians and the Syrians, and on the other side the Americans and the Israelis," he said. "And we are in the middle. We had a dream of an independent Lebanon, we had a dream of stability, and now it's a shambles."

Journalist Riad Ali expected Israel's Arab population to adopt an independent stand in the conflict, just as Jumblatt does, and not blindly follow the militant voices. "It is time that they decide where they are, not for the sake of the Jews but for their own sake, for the sake of the values they want to give their children.... It is clear to all that a Palestinian state headed by Hamas and a Lebanon under the reign of Hezbollah are not the frameworks which will grow democratic societies with social and political pluralism. It is clear that under such regimes, the rule of law, human rights, the freedom of religious worship, religion, women's rights, freedom of movement, freedom of expression and thought, etc., are considered alien and ridicu-lous notions, to say the least."

If anything, the war with Hezbollah has estranged the Druze minority further from the Arab minority, leaving Israel with an even more complex communal puzzle than before.

THE GOLAN DRUZE

BEFORE PROCEEDING ANY FURTHER WITH the discussion on the Druze in Israel proper, a few words need to be said about the Druze in the Golan, the northern part of the country that was taken from Syria in the Six-Day War and officially annexed to Israel in 1981. On one hand, one cannot ignore the Druze of the Golan in a book on the Druze in Israel. After all, they are Israeli inhabitants. On the other hand, they are very different from their brethren from pre-1967 Israel. Whereas the Druze in the Carmel and Galilee are proud Israeli citizens, the Druze of the Golan claim to be Syrian citizens—in other words, citizens of an enemy country.

Despite this stated position, however, the Golan Druze are certainly Israel's friendliest enemies. Israelis who visit the Golan (often on their way to the ski resort on Mt. Hermon) are greeted warmly in the four Druze villages in the Golan. The local restaurants are full, just like in Daliat al-Carmel. Never has any harm been done to an Israeli in the Golan, while the number of Golan Druze ever convicted of hostile action is negligible. Indeed, for the first ten years after the 1967 occupation of that area, the Golan Druze were considered the least problematic of the populations that had come under Israeli rule. Access to Israel provided them with previously unavailable work opportunities, tourism prospered, and the Golan Druze enjoyed an unprecedented economic boom.

Paradoxically, it was after the historic visit of Egyptian

President Anwar Sadat to Israel in November 1977 that caused the Golan Druze to reevaluate their relationship with Israel. The Druze were concerned that perhaps they had taken their amicable relations with the Jews one step too far. Although President Hafez al-Assad of Syria was one of the strongest critics of Sadat's move, the Druze feared that this new era of Israeli–Arab compromise could lead Israel one day to withdraw from the Golan, just as it was about to withdraw from Egyptian Sinai. Once that happened and the lands of the Golan Druze were again under Syrian rule, they feared the Syrians would settle accounts with those who had identified with Israel.

The Druze revolted when four years later the Knesset virtually annexed the Golan by passing a bill extending Israeli law over the Golan and demanding that all Druze accept Israeli citizenship. Maj. Gen. Amir Drori, the officer in charge of the IDF's northern command, became nervous. He received orders to move his headquarters from the Galilee to the Golan Heights to demonstrate Israel's determination to proceed with the annexation act. Nonetheless, he felt uneasy about exercising force against the hitherto friendly Golan Druze.

"Your 'buddies' are running wild," he told Dr. Nissim Dana. "Why don't you talk to them and find out what's happening?" Dana, a veteran student of the Arab society and Arab culture, was the official in charge of non-Jewish communities at the ministry of religious affairs.

"I met their religious leader, Sheikh Salman Taher abu-Seleh," Dana recalled. "We chatted for an hour on everything else but the real issue. When he finally asked about the reason for my visit, I told him I needed to understand why the Druze had acted so strongly."

"I will tell you one thing," the old sheikh told the Israeli official. "When your government decides what it wants in the

Golan Heights, let us know and we will follow you blindly." The Golan Druze did not believe that Israel was *really* determined to hold onto that territory for eternity.

"When you speak of a compromise," the Druze leader explained, "we are the ones who will pay the price for every compromise, because the border of our village is the border with Syria. How do you want me to act, knowing that with the first possible agreement with Syria, our village will be handed over to the Syrians? If we openly acquiesce to the Israeli annex-ation, the Syrians will demand explanations, and there is no High Court of Justice in Damascus. We do not hate you, but I need to protect my community. We must take care of ourselves, because nobody else will."

In the end, their gut feeling was right. Several Israeli gov-ernments have sent out feelers for negotiations of a territorial compromise with Syria, although no real negotiations have materialized. The same political reality existed at the time this book was written in 2006. Yes, the Druze of the Golan are the same hospitable people, many work in Israel proper, many speak Hebrew fluently, many will say ("between me and you") that they would prefer the Israeli rule to the Syrian one. However, twenty-five years after the annexation of the Golan, the fears are still there. Thus, essentially the Druze of the Golan—in sharp contrast to their brethren in the Galilee and the Carmel—are proud Syrians. Until further notice.

DRUZE IN THE ARMY

ALTHOUGH THE DRUZE IN THE Middle East had often used the practice of *a-takkiya*, underplaying their communal identity and merging with mainstream society whenever their existence was threatened, whenever they did take to the battlefield, they fought courageously. "When suffering, they burst out like crazy," said professor Mansour. The best example in recent history is the uprising of Druze tribes throughout Syria and in part of Lebanon against French mandatory officials who attempted to upset the traditions and the tribal hierarchy of Jabel a-Druze in Syria. Though the Druze fought "like crazy," however, they lost the battle, and the French mandatory authorities eventually suppressed the revolt. Samih Natour and Akram Hasson noted in their book *The Druze* that the 1925 revolt elevated Druze prestige among the Syrians and within the Arab world. They gained a reputation of being a small community capable of handling big operations. This fact assisted them greatly after Syria gained its independence. It also became the core of the unique alliance between the Druze and the Jewish state.

As early as April 1948, a month before the establishment of the Jewish state, young Druze joined the Haganah, the pre-state Jewish military organization, During Israel's War of Independence, it was only natural for the Druze community to side with the Jews and, in 1956, the Druze leadership accepted compulsory military service. Until the beginning of the 1970s, most Druze had served in Unit 300, a special minorities' unit, but they have gradually integrated into all units. In the past fifty years, the Druze have demonstrated their skill as soldiers while serving in the ranks of the Israel Defense Forces.

A special Druze division was formed in 1979, with Col. Hail Salah from the village of Mughar appointed the first Druze division commander. Nevertheless, Druze conscripts were free to serve in other units as well.

The Druze have earned their right to be full members of the Israeli society the hard way. In a country overburdened with bloodshed and bereavement, in some Druze villages the ratio of fallen soldiers exceeds the national figures. By the beginning of 2006, residents of the Galilee village of Beit Jann had buried fifty-six of their sons who had fallen in battle. Fifty-six, out of a population of ten thousand, is more than 0.5 percent. The Druze have lost some 340 of their sons in Israel's wars, leaving behind 107 widows and 375 orphans. Alas, one cannot measure the pain in percentages, even in a fraction of a percent. These numbers need to be remembered; compared to the population as a whole, the Druze have sacrificed for Israel's security more than anyone else.

On the western outskirts of Daliat al-Carmel we meet a former member of the Knesset who paid that painful price. He is Amal Nasser a-Din, the father of Lutfi, whose incarnated soul we met in the body of Wissam in the village of Sajour. Amal Nasser a-Din is the chairperson of Yad Labanim, the association commemorating the fallen Druze soldiers. He relives the loss of his son every day. Moreover, since Lutfi's death, Amal lost another son under mysterious circumstances.

The driveway to the main office looks like a path into the past. A huge gateway opens up to a scenic garden. At its center stands a 120-year-old building of aristocratic appearance, constructed by Sir Lawrence Oliphant (1829–1888), the distinguished English traveler who was among the earliest Christian sympathizers of the nascent Zionist movement. It was here, say the Druze, that Sir Lawrence's secretary, Naftali Hertz-Imber, wrote "Hatikva," which eventually became Israel's national anthem.

Meeting with Amal was indeed a journey into the past—a reunion of sorts with his fallen sons and with the other sons who had fallen in Israel's battles. Amal greeted us in a huge room on the first floor of the building, which was decorated with both the national flag of Israel and the Druze flag, surrounded by pictures of young Druze who had fallen in battle. Memories of the past have become part of his daily routine; as if his own bereavement were not painful enough, he copes daily with the pains of others.

Amal Nasser a-Din is the father of four boys and two girls. Two of the boys live no more. There was no pain in his voice as he recounted the story of his losses. His eyes were shining, and his mouth kept a certain smile as he spoke slowly, recalling the days of his bereavement.

"Some thirty thousand people came to the funeral of Lutfi. I swore that I wouldn't break down. I knew then, and I know now; this is a price that needs to be paid. The Druze have never had their own state, the Druze have never had a safe place. I believe that the State of Israel is the best solution for the Druze. It is the only place in the world where they enjoy full freedom. The Jews are the only people in the world whose trust in the Druze is unconditional. Sending our boys to the army is a price we must pay. At times the price is much higher; the highest price a parent can pay."

Amal recuperated and served three terms as Member of the

Playground donated by the Everett Foundation.

Knesset, representing the Likud ruling party. Seventeen years later, Amal lost another son. His son Saleh was kidnapped while shopping in the West Bank town of Jenin and has not been heard of since. There have been no demands for prisoner exchange or ransom, and no one has claimed responsibility for the kidnapping. Nothing. The young man, twenty-six years old and the father of three children, simply disappeared. Amal has no doubt that his son's kidnappers knew exactly who his father was. Every now and then Amal writes a letter to the defense minister asking whether there is any progress in the investigation. The answer is always the same: "We are pursuing the matter."

Amal, whose Druze pride is painted with the strong colors of Zionist pride, represents the general mood in the community. The Druze, like most Israelis, may at times be very critical of the government, but they, too, share the "my country, right or wrong" approach to the state.

"A Druze must serve his country, no matter where he lives," said one soldier, as we interrupted the training of a platoon of Druze soldiers in the Negev, nudging them with our questions. "I live in this country, so I must defend it."

We also met a Druze air force navigator, the one they named Ayin, an acronym for his private name (the names of Israeli pilots are classified for security reasons). In his modest manner he, too, burst with pride at being the first in the clan to fly those powerful birds, Israel's security blanket.

Not everyone shares the conviction; not every one serves. Some Druze youths refused to serve in the army on principle, feeling more loyal to their Arab ethnic origins than to their country. At times they go to jail rather than be drafted; other times they will find roundabout ways to avoid the draft. As early as 1972, a group of young Druze formed the "Initiative Committee" of Druze draft objectors. Druze poet and writer Salman Natour, a founder of the group, argues that Druze should refuse to serve in the army "because they are part of the Palestinian minority in Israel and cannot take part in operations of an army which fights against themselves."

Salman was one of twelve Druze students whose military service was deferred in favor of university studies. However, after graduating from the Hebrew University in 1971, Salman and his friends received army enlistment orders. Most of them abided, but Salman refused. He spent twelve days in a military prison and seven days on a hunger strike, but eventually gave in. The system was stronger. He served in a Druze village as a soldier-teacher.

"I object to the draft, because I feel that there is no reason to serve. I am not willing to serve in a society that does not give me equal rights. Moreover, it is immoral to demand from us, as Palestinian Arabs, that we serve in an army whose purpose is to fight our people. There is something immoral in taking non-Jews to die for this country." Unlike many Druze, Salman does not perceive the Druze as a separate ethnic group within Israel's Arab population. "I am a Palestinian Arab," he declares.

It was during Salman's military service that he wrote his best-selling book (in Arabic) *Anta al-Katel ya Sheikh* ("You are the Murderer, Sheikh"). It is a novel about a soldier from Salman's village of Daliat al-Carmel who, during the 1973 Yom Kippur War, kills his brother-in-law on the Syrian side of the front.

His loyalty to the Palestinian cause is total, regardless of the ugly divisions of the Palestinian national struggle.

"Three years ago my wife's nephew Kamar, thirteen, was killed in a suicide bombing at a Haifa bus stop. It is still very painful, but I cannot change my views on the occupation. I do not cope with life with sentiments. My solidarity with the struggle of the Palestinians is not because I am Palestinian, but because I am against occupation and oppression. My views are more moral than political. I am a person who strives to be a moral person. The moral dictate is to reject oppression, but at the same time I am against the murder of people.

"I don't feel myself an Israeli. True, my identity comprises Israeli elements; I speak Hebrew and was influenced by the culture, and I do not reject them. I wish I had five more cultures, but I am not Israeli in my being. I don't accept the Jewish identity of the state. I want to change it in a political way, so that it will be a democratic state for all its citizens."

On this point, Salman has taken another step away from his Communist heritage. Israel's Communist party was one of the first to coin the slogan "two countries for two peoples": Israel for the Jews and Palestine for the Arabs.

Salman is aware of the paradox between his old, Communist credo and the belief that Israel should be stripped of its Jewish character. His way out of the dilemma: "The two-state solution is only an interim stage in which both peoples will work out an agreed pattern for one, common country. Perhaps the pattern is one that hasn't been found yet.

"Yesterday I had guests from Torino, Italy. They told me about some 380,000 Germans living in South Tirol in northern Italy. They enjoy full autonomy, so that some ninety-five percent of their taxes stay there. The Italians regard their German minority as a national treasure. I wish the Israelis would treat us as a national treasure. For many Israelis, we are a national nuisance.

"Look at me, when I began speaking up, contrary to most Druze, I was arrested because I played a different music. During my Communist days, I was arrested for forty-eight hours without trial, interrogated by a General Security Service agent by the name of Gideon Ezra [he was minister of internal security at the time]. They interrogated me on my book and other writings and tried to seduce me into quitting the Communist party and breaking the anti-draft Initiative Committee into pieces. I refused to cooperate and told them they had no incriminating evidence against me and would need to let me go. Indeed they did."

Salman's children have followed his example. None of them has served in the army.

"I wrote the army that I do not want my children to serve in the army. I raised them as Palestinian Arabs, and thus they should not serve in the Israeli army."

What if any of them would have insisted on enlisting?

"I would have respected their choice, but none of them

would have entered my house in an IDF uniform. I would not intervene, but I would have thought that something was wrong in my education of them."

Natour argues that as many as sixty percent of young Druze are draft dodgers, but there is no way to check that number since the army does not release figures on its conscripts, especially according to communal affiliation. Military sources reject that figure, however, saying that the scope of draft dodgers is minimal. "According to army figures, Druze youths demonstrate a high level of motivation to serve, particularly in combat units," said military sources.

Three Druze organizations are currently campaigning to exempt Druze youths from military service. Jihad Sa'ad, secretary of the Initiative Committee against compulsory service, said that their call has become increasingly effective, and that more and more Druze youngsters try to evade military service. "Compulsory service did not bring us any progress. The Druze community is just as neglected as the Arab community, which is exempt of military service," Sa'ad told us. "We prefer that rather than serving three years in the army; our youngsters invest their time in education."

However, my impression is that the vast majority of the Druze take the opposite view. They believe that fulfilling their civilian duties gives them the legitimacy to demand a just share of the national cake, including industrialization of the Druze villages, a richer choice of work opportunities, more job openings in the civil service, and most of all a better school system.

One Druze soldier commented, "Rights and duties, that is the name of the game. Serving in the army is my duty. I receive and I contribute."

"I will go to the army out of choice," said Ayal Mansour of Issfiya, sixteen. "Most of my friends want to go to the army."

This contention is supported by Dr. Nissim Dana and Dr. Shimon Avivi, both of whom have studied the Druze community thoroughly. They claim that a high proportion, some eighty-six percent of Druze eighteen year olds, go into the army, a rate that is even higher than among the Jews of conscription age. Some thirty percent of the Jews manage to avoid the draft each year.

Nissim Dana joined the civil service in 1963 as liaison officer with the Druze community. Soon after he entered office, he convinced the defense establishment to exempt young religious Druze from compulsory military service, similar to the exemption given to young orthodox Jews. The orthodox Jews have taken advantage of the exemption in steadily growing numbers, however, whereas the number of Druze who study religion instead of serving in the army does not exceed a hundred a year.

Palestinians are usually indifferent to the alliance between the Jews and the Druze. They regard it as a fact that would be difficult to change in the foreseeable future. At one point, a group of Arab security prisoners sent an open letter to the Druze leadership in Israel, warning that relations between the Druze and the Palestinians might lead to an open confrontation between the two communities. The prisoners' main grievance was their maltreatment by Druze wardens. They called for their collective resignation and demanded an official Druze apology before the Palestinian people. "The only enemy must be the occupation," wrote the prisoners. Nothing happened. The Druze continue to serve in the army, the border police, and the prisons service.

On the face of it, the military service is the culmination of Druze integration with the Jewish majority. Not only do young Druze share a "blood bond" with their Jewish mates, but they

Dr. Ruth with an Israeli Druze soldier in a jeep.

are also exposed to the temptations offered by the relatively liberal and open Jewish society. For the first time, Druze youth live outside the hub of their villages and extended families. They enjoy military machismo, freedom of movement and behavior—away from the watchful eyes of family—and exposure to relatively liberal relations with Jewish girls.

So where does the border run? If you date a Jewish girl, you may end up marrying her. How lovely, an outside observer may think, if those two peoples share a "blood bond," why not share a "love bond"?

"If I date or marry a Jewish girl, my family will abandon me. It's as simple as that," said Ayin, the air force navigator. "They'll have nothing to do with me. I can enjoy Jewish friends, have fun, have a drink, and meet girls, but in the end I remember my home and family. Ultimately my home is what I am.

The bottom line is being Druze, marrying a Druze woman, and raising a family to carry on the line."

Alas, Ayin draws a picture that is too good to be true. The temptations are there, and many cannot resist them. Many do cross the line and taste the forbidden fruits, hoping that no one will notice or, better yet, that the people at home will shut their eyes. The temptations are there, and they make the challenge so much more difficult. And the challenge is great—to get full exposure to the Israeli society while maintaining the tribe and its customs; to live side by side with Jewish and Arab neighbors and share their values, and yet preserve one's Druze identity.

DRUZE AND ARABS

DRUZE *ARE* ARABS, YET MANY of them would like to forget it. They speak Arabic, and their ethnic origins are Arab. They used to share the same religion until they split away from the mother religion. In fact, it is a mistake to speak of Druze *and* Arabs. Druze living in Lebanon perceive themselves as members of the Arab Lebanese nation, Druze living in Syria, are Arab Syrians, and Druze living in Israel are ... well, part of the Israeli Arab community. In their religious creed and in their political alliance with Zionism, the Druze in Israel differ from the larger Arab community. They differ from their brethren in the Arab countries, because they are the only Druze community in the region that identifies itself as purely Druze.

It was 1970 when a young Druze member of the Labor Party begged Premier Golda Meir, leader of the party, to separate the Druze members from the Arab department in the party. Amal Nasser a-Din served as a spokesperson on behalf of those Druze who did not want to be associated with the Arabs in any way, wanting instead to be integrated into Israel's ruling party with the same status as its Jewish members.

Golda appointed a committee to review the request and its political implications. "We have a serious problem with our youths," Amal told the committee, "we are not Arabs. Arabism was forced on us." The committee turned down Amal's request. "Our Arab friends will be insulted," was their expressed concern.

Amal was fed up with hypocrisy. He quit the Labor Party,

and joined the opposition Likud Party, bringing thousands of Druze voters with him. Seven years later, he became the first Druze Knesset member on the Likud list.

His former political home, the Labor Party, eventually adopted his position. Not only did it separate the Druze from the Arabs but also abolished the Arab department altogether. Party apartheid ended, but the tension continued. The crux of the matter is the fact that the Druze serve in the army and the other Arabs don't. The Arabs regard the Druze as "collaborators" with the Zionist state. At the same time, however, they envy the Druze for their full integration into the Israeli society. Arab hostility toward the Druze of Israel is widespread. Israeli Druze visiting Jordan and Egypt rarely introduce themselves as Druze, but as Arabs. Druze who live in Saudi Arabia, for example, live underground. They are forced to put on Sunni attire; they pretend to be Sunni Muslims, but deep inside they are Druze. Remember, the Druze culture allows the use of *takkiya*—hiding one's communal identity in times of stress—as a means of survival.

Survival, that's the name of the game, and it is not an easy task. When young Druze men, who were exposed to Western values during their military service, return home, they neither fully enjoy the benefits of the Western Israeli society, nor do they live completely with the traditional values. They are stuck in between. They suffer unemployment while many of the Arabs with whom they shared a high school classroom have completed their university studies. This contributes to frustration and hurts relations with both the Israeli establishment and Arab neighbors. Azzam Azzam, an Israeli Druze textile worker from the village of Mughar, served eight years in an Egyptian prison on apparently false charges of espionage. Another, Riad Ali of the same village, was kidnapped and almost murdered.

On a bright September day in 2004, a white car pulled in front of a taxi in a Gaza street, blocking its way. A man in his early twenties, dressed in civilian clothes, emerged from the car, stuck a revolver through the taxi window, and said in Arabic, "Which one of you is Riad?"

The passengers, members of a CNN television news team, were dumbstruck at first, but then one of them said, "I am Riad." Riad Ali, then forty-two, had worked for two years as a producer for CNN.

Two other men got out of the intercepting car, carrying AK-47 assault rifles, forced Ali at gunpoint into their car, and drove away. Ali was held captive for twenty-four hours and released unharmed after heavy pressure, which involved Palestinian President Yasser Arafat in person. The exact circumstances of the abduction still remain vague. Ali refuses to elaborate, but it is quite clear that the abductors were well aware of Ali's ethnic background.

Shortly before his release, a videotape surfaced in which Ali explained he was being held by the Al-Aksa Martyrs' Brigades, a militant offshoot of Arafat's Fatah movement. On the tape, Ali explained in Arabic that he is a Druze Arab, and that his father and other members of his family have served in the Israeli military. Ali himself did not serve. His enlistment date came shortly after Israel's invasion of Lebanon. As a gesture of protest against the invasion, Ali had refused to serve.

On the video, which was recorded while he was held captive, Ali called for the Druze not to serve in the Israeli military, saying that the Druze should share the Palestinian cause. Riad was eventually released, thanks to the direct intervention of President Yasser Arafat. After his release, one of Riad's first comments was to thank Arafat.

A week after Riad Ali's abduction, we were invited to celebrate his release. It was a demonstration of Druze strength. At times it seemed as if the entire Druze community had decided to come. An endless queue of people in this predominantly Druze village of Mughar came through the backyard of Sa'id Ghanem's residence to share his joy over the release of his son.

Now, finally at home, protected within the warm embrace of his family and the entire Druze community, Riad was visibly moved by the hundreds, not to say thousands, who came to celebrate his release. They came from all villages, young and old, clergymen dressed with their long robes and headscarves, soldiers and conscientious objectors. They hugged and kissed Riad and his father, and then took a seat on one of dozens of chairs lined up around the courtyard. Riad hardly had time to talk to anyone. The guests kept coming and coming.

"At times of need, we are all one," said a retired army lieutenant colonel, the Ghanems' next-door neighbor and a family relative. "As soon as we heard that Riad was abducted, everyone rushed here to offer help. We were determined not to let go until Riad's safe return."

The incident accentuated the Druze dilemma between their Arab heritage and their Israeli identity. Likud Knesset Member Majali Wihbeh warned the Palestinians not to kidnap any more members of the Druze community. "They are opening a front which could develop into a difficult chapter of bloodshed. We, as Druze, will know how to cope with them."

Another Druze Likud Knesset Member, Ayoub Kara, said he was not surprised by the kidnapping. "Ever since the outbreak of the Intifada, the Palestinians try to draw a wedge between the Druze community and the State of Israel, urging the Druze not to serve in the army because of their Arab ethnic origin," Kara said. "We serve willingly because we appreciate living in a democratic country which unlike the neighboring countries is willing to confront tyranny and radical Islamization."

However, said Likud Knesset Member Kara, the kidnapping of the Druze journalist only strengthened Druze ties with Israel. "We prefer to live here, in a country where no one abducts journalists, be they Druze or others," Kara said.

The subtitle of *a-Duha* ("Sunrise"), a Druze newspaper in Lebanon, reads: "An Islamic Druze Journal." The adjective "Islamic" is added to stress the Islamic origin of the Druze in a country that, for centuries, has known a merry-go-round of conflicts between Druze and Muslims, Druze and Christians, and Christians and Muslims.

Lebanon almost managed to cause a deep rift between the Druze and the Jews. When Israel invaded Lebanon in 1982, Israeli Druze were swept with happiness: Finally the border to their brethren in the north was opened up. Families could be reunited; old friendships could be renewed.

Samih Natour, sixty, a newspaper and encyclopedias publisher, also of Daliat al-Carmel, founded a periodical he named *al-Imama* (named for the white turban that Druze men wrap their faces with). "I thought that this would be an opportunity to open up to our brethren in Syria and Lebanon." Then came the disenchantment, however. Israeli's incursion into Lebanon turned into a lengthy occupation. The Druze in Lebanon blamed the Israeli soldiers for siding with the Christians at their account, and the Druze in Israel sided with them, demonstrating against the Israeli army's involvement in Lebanon, and threatening to break the old blood bondage between the Druze and the Jews.

Thanks to those Druze demonstrations, further deployment of the Christian forces in the predominantly Shouf Mountains was prevented.

Luckily Israel's forces withdrew to the south of Lebanon, before relations between the Druze and the Jews deteriorated further.

* * *

Samih is the brother of Salman Natour, the poet, who stands at the forefront of those demanding to exempt Israel's Druze from military service. Two opposites in the same family. Samih is the father of six children, four boys and two girls. The girls are married and live in their own houses; two of the boys are still at home. The pride of the family is Izar, twenty years old and a graduate of the IDF Junior Command Preparatory School in Haifa, and an officer excelling in the Givati brigade. Samih proudly displays the certificate of excellence on the bookshelf in the living room. It cannot be missed.

The Natours go back some three hundred years to trace their origins in Lebanon. Three brothers of the respectable Dhau family left the village of Zaroun, northeast of Beirut, following bloody struggles with their Christian-Maronite neighbors. They actually fled for their lives, emigrating south to Palestine. One brother settled in the northern Galilee village of Beit Jann, the other in the Lower Galilee village of Mughar, and the third settled in Shalalah, a Druze village just south of Haifa. They called him Zarouni, after his original home village in Lebanon.

Some eighteen Druze villages prospered on Mt. Carmel at the beginning of the nineteenth century. However, when Egyptian warlord Ibrahim Pasha returned from an unfortunate confrontation with Druze warriors on Jabel Druze in Syria, he took revenge for his defeat through punitive measures against the Druze on Mt. Carmel. Sixteen villages were destroyed by fire. Only Daliat al-Carmel and Issfiya survived the attack and lasted to this very day.

Samih's great-grandfather lost his land in the attack, after which he made his living as the guard of the village. The Arabic word *Natour* means "guard," hence the family's present name. Only a splinter of the giant Dhau family in Lebanon remained on Mt. Carmel. As a minority within the Druze society, the Natours devoted much time and energy to education.

As late as the 1940s, most Druze villagers were illiterate. The Natour family was the exception. Four members of the family became well-known poets, including Nayef Natour, Samih's father. During the 1950s, he made a living writing intercession letters to the authorities on behalf of his neighbors. "We are an educated family. I was the first Dalia resident who was a student at the Hebrew University in Jerusalem."

Another brother, Shehadeh, is an expert on Arabic, Hebrew and poetry. Amin, the youngest, is a musician, who specializes in the rejuvenation of Druze music.

Al-Imama is still published periodically, and it often makes the entire trip from Daliat al-Carmel to Damascus. "When I first published the paper in 1982, I expected the Druze in Lebanon to contribute." Natour thought the exposure to the free Israeli press would trigger his Lebanese brethren to write freely. He was in for disappointment. The Druze of Lebanon did not dare write in an Israeli paper, even though it was in Arabic and in the communal press. At least the authorities, in both Lebanon and Syria, do not ban the distribution of the Druze newspaper. Syria's President Bashar al-Assad reportedly gave Sheikh Muwafak Tarif, the spiritual head of the community in Israel, the green light to send copies to Syria.

This does not mean, however, that Israeli Druze have received Arab rehabilitation. Largely, the Arabs, both in Israel and in the neighboring Arab countries regard the Druze as collaborators with their Zionist enemy. Samih is well aware of those Israeli Druze who hide their Druze identity when visiting Arab countries. Those Arabs simply do not understand the Druze, claims Samih Natour. The Druze do not identify with Israel because it is a stronger party, but because Druze always identify with their host country. "It is not that the Druze side with the stronger party, but rather that the Druze are the main reason that the strong party is strong," argued Natour.

When Amir Abdullah founded the Arab Emirate of Transjordan in 1922, he appointed Rashid Teli'a, a Lebanese Druze, as his first prime minister. Sultan al-Atrash, leader of the Druze Revolt against the French in Syria in 1925, is considered a national hero in Syria, as one of the main contributors to its independence some twenty years later.

In Lebanon, local Druze leader Amir Majid Arslan was the first to raise Lebanon's national flag upon its independence in 1946.

The officer who was in charge of the home front in Israel during the Second Gulf War was Maj. Gen. Yussuf Mishlib, the highest ranking Druze officer. The commander of Israel's border police force is also a Druze, Maj. Gen. Hussein Farres from the village of Hurfesh in upper Galilee.

* * *

The village of Mughar, home to journalist Riad Ali and Azzam Azzam, who spent eight years in an Egyptian prison on espionage charges, emerged in the news once again in 2005.

For two days, on February 12 and 13, 2005, the Christians in Mughar suffered a virtual pogrom, committed by young Druze. The perpetrators were hooligans, but the riots exposed an ugly scar on the face of the Druze community. Young Druze stoned Christian neighbors, smashed and burned their cars, burst into houses, and vandalized their belongings. Eleven people were injured, including three police officers, but everyone shared in the trauma.

Following the riots, many Christians left the village and sought shelter in other Arab villages in the Galilee. Many compared the events in Mughar to the German *Kristallnacht* against Jews in 1938. The village elders were unable to restrain the young hooligans. "For fifty years we have nurtured our relations," lamented Kamal Ghanem, himself a Druze, "and it was all destroyed in one day."

It was the explosive formula of religion, honor—and sex— that ignited the riots. The immediate reason for the pogrom was a rumor spread by one young Druze that Christian youths had placed pictures of nude Druze girls on the Internet. It was said that, by means of photomontage, a Christian had attached pictures of nude bodies to the faces of real Druze girls. The rumor spread fast, and violence spread even faster—although, at the end of the day, the rumor proved to be false, a hoax. Essentially, however, this did not really matter. The explosive tinder was already present, and only the spark was missing. "They would have found another reason to strike," said Riad Ali, the journalist.

Half of the twenty thousand residents of Mughar are Druze, the other half are Christian and Muslim Arabs. The story goes that, when the IDF entered the village during the War of Independence in 1948, the Israeli commander wanted to separate the Druze, Muslims, and Christian Arabs. However, the Druze village head, Hussein Araideh, faced the Israeli commander and told him, "We are all one," thus saving his non-Druze neighbors the trauma of becoming refugees like 600,000 other Palestinians. On the surface, relations between these three Arab communities are still relatively good. However, from time to time, sparks of inter-communal hatred and suspicion turn into flames of violence. This time around, violence reached a new peak. Luckily no one was killed.

The crux of the problem is that young Druze serve three years of compulsory military service, just like any Jewish citizen of Israel, which creates a gap between them and their Christian and Muslim neighbors. Once young Druze complete their military service, they often return home to face growing unemployment. Unemployment in the Druze villages runs higher than the national average. While young Druze serve the country, their Arab counterparts can complete university studies. "Obviously, the employer will prefer an Arab educated person over a Druze who has just come out of the army," said Likud Knesset Member Ayoub Kara.

Not only are the Christians better educated, but they are also better off economically. They have the churches behind them as institutions that provide not only religious services, but also educational and welfare services. They have the Vatican. The Druze, on the other hand, despite their "blood alliance" with the Jews, feel frustrated and neglected and have a weak leadership—no one was able to step into the shoes of the legendary Sheikh Amin Tarif, the spiritual head of the community, who died in 1993 at the age of ninety-five. Their villages have no industry, no work, insufficient housing for young couples, and a poor educational system.

Young Druze men are exposed to Western values during their military service, and when they return home, they can neither enjoy the benefits of the Western Israeli society, nor can they live with the traditional values. They are stuck in the middle. The result is frustration, which was directed at their Christian neighbors that day.

Thus, the tragic events of Mughar should not be seen as an isolated incident but as part of a puzzle of fragile relations between the non-Jewish communities in Israel. Moreover, some argued that it was a projection of the tense relationship between Druze and Christians in Lebanon, Israel's neighbor on the north. Relations between Israel and its Druze community suffered a serious blow during the Lebanon War (1982–1983), when local Druze complained that Israel had sided with the Christians of Lebanon because of the Lebanese Druze community.

"Nonsense," said Professor Keis Firro, a Druze historian, of Haifa University, "there is no connection. The political context in Lebanon is totally different; the regime is communal, and the Druze have a totally different role in Lebanese politics."

Firro determined that the root of the violence was a question of identity. "In Israel, the Druze are perceived as neither Arabs nor Jews." The national hero's welcome given to Azzam Azzam, the Druze who was held in Egyptian prison on false charges of being an Israeli spy, deepened the rift with the Arab community. When Azzam covered himself proudly with the national flag, it was as if the entire community did the same, increasing the suspicion of the Arabs in Israel, said Firro. The result is growing frustration. The riots that erupted in Mughar between Druze and Christians are an expression of that frustration.

"Not all of our youngsters go to universities after the military service," said Riad Ali. "Many return home with Western values, but they don't actually have a real education. While they were serving in the army, their Muslim and the Christian neighbors either studied or began working, got married, and began building their lives. The Druze veteran returns home to find that the community leadership is held by Christians and Muslims. The Druze army veterans desperately try to fill in the three-year gap, but they are often stuck and even unemployed. They can become extremely jealous of their non-Druze neighbors. They often feel inferior to those who contributed nothing to the state security. They feel the need to do something to compensate for their inferiority.

"The riots in Mughar were an attempt by frustrated young Druze to make their neighbors pay for their impotence; to make them concede—if need be, by force—that the Druze are superior to them. This is the way to translate the illusion of power into net power."

A week after the riots, there was still tension in the village. Dozens of police patrols were seen on the winding alleys of this picturesque mountain village, as a local appeasement (*sulha*) committee was trying to find a formula that would end hostilities.

The next Sunday, the church bells tolled in solidarity with the Christians who were hurt in the riots, as dignitaries arrived for Sunday services. Never before had the small church in the Galilee village of Mughar seen so many important guests, starring the Vatican's representative in Israel, Msgr. Pietro Sambi. Apostolic delegate Sambi said that the village had become the center of world attention following the "difficult events." Rather than putting the blame on the Druze hooligans, however, he blamed the Israeli police for failing to protect the Christians in Mughar.

Local Christians charged that police had failed to cut down the scope of violence, because so many of the Druze residents were members of the security forces, and they did not dare confront them.

Zuheir Andreus, editor of the Arabic weekly *Kul al-Arab*, suggested that the events in Mughar were yet another manifestation of the long-term policy of the government to put a wedge between the non-Jewish communities, turning one against the other. Professor Firro rejected that theory, as well, but in his book *The Druzes in the Jewish State: A Brief History* (1999), he cited documents indicating a continuous government trend, whose exact aim had been to separate the Druze and the Arabs and to widen the split among the Arabs themselves.

"There is no doubt that the Druze have gone too far," said Professor Firro. "As a Druze, I am ashamed. How can you punish a whole community for the folly of several youths? I blame not only the hooligans, but those who did not stop it."

Firro added, however, that this was no isolated incident but part of the general "lunacy" in the Middle East, which is often so difficult to control.

Boy Meets Girl

During the summer of 2005, my documentary crew and I returned to the tormented village of Mughar to meet local youths who were not yet old enough to have been drafted, who had fewer years of communal prejudice, and who were therefore less occupied with communal differences—and more with common teenage issues. We wanted to talk to them *before* the Druze boys go to the army; before their encounter with the outside world.

Indeed, on the face of it, the group of high-school youths we met at the local youth center looked like young people almost anywhere else in the world. Some of them—girls and boys—wore jeans and fashionable shirts and were aware of their good looks. They were fully cognizant of the latest fashions, rock hits, school gossip, and whatever other qualifications are needed to be an up-to-date teenager. They discussed events in their village openly, disassociating themselves from the hooligans, and analyzed the latest political developments with admirable insights. Their conversation might be typical of any teenagers—until we reached the subject that's on top of the agenda of boys and girls at that age: the issue of "boy meets girl." Suddenly they put on their traditional, conservative, family-tradition attire. We found no rebels, no pioneers.

"What happens if you want to go out at night?" I asked the girls.

Dr. Ruth with Druze high school students at Mughar youth center.

"You mean with boys? The answer is No."

"Can you go out with girls?"

"Yes, but not at night."

"What if you want to go out, but mother says no?"

"You stay home."

"What if you want to go out with friends to the city?"

"Within the village we are free, but to go to the nearby town of Tiberias or to Tel-Aviv, you can go only with mother or father or on a school trip; there is always a chaperone. We don't go out on our own."

"What if mother says 'okay' and father says 'no'?"

"Then it's 'no.'"

"What if father says 'yes' and mother says 'no'?"

"The man always has the last word."

"The man? When you get married, will it be like that in your family?"

"Yes, of course."

This may all sound very nice. Here are youths who demonstrate obedience to their parents, follow family and tribal rules, and know their limits—just like in the good old times. Tradition is still strong enough to make these young people conform—despite all the outside temptations. Nevertheless, this is only part of the picture. Many young Druze want to break out of this shell, say goodbye to old traditions, and be like the others. The elder, conservative Druze are aware of the trend and would like to avert it. They are concerned that the future of the community might be at stake.

Leaders of the Druze society are even more sensitive about assimilation than are the Jews in the Diaspora. The one major objection is intermarriage. Marrying a non-Druze, whether Jewish, Muslim, Christian, or a member of any other creed, usually means excommunication. The violator might be excommunicated not only from the society as a whole, but even from the immediate family. This shows not only the great influence of religious leadership, but also the immense power of traditional values—despite the open, Western society in which the Druze live and despite the change of times.

Even Lt. Ayin, the air force navigator, the one for whom integration into the Israeli society the sky is literally the limit, understands his limitations and has accepted them. "I can enjoy the mainstream and still retain my Druze values," he told us. "I can enjoy Jewish friends, have fun, have a drink, and meet girls, but in the end I remember my home and family. If I date or marry a Jewish girl, my family will abandon me; it's as simple as that. They will have nothing to do with me."

The ban on mixed marriages is total, for men and women

alike. Men who marry non-Druze women suffer severe sanctions. The "sinner" is considered an outcast. He might be banned from entering his home village, deprived of family inheritance, and, worst of all, his children are no longer considered Druze and forbidden to marry a Druze. Such sanctions are mild, however, compared to the punishment of women who choose to wed out-of-tribe.

"For a Druze woman to marry a non-Druze man is tantamount to a self-imposed death sentence," says Dr. Nissim Dana. Dana knows the Druze inside out. Until 2002, he served for years as director of the division for religious communities at the ministry of religions. He has also studied them from his academic position at Haifa University. Dana's latest book, *The Druze in the Middle East: Their Faith, Leadership, Identity, and Status* (2003), is an attempt to fill in the gap on the Druze.

"I feared the reactions to my book, both of the clergymen, for having openly dealt with the Druze faith, and also the Druze Arab nationalists, who would certainly say that this was an attempt to draw a wedge between the Druze and the larger Arab community.

"But the reactions were favorable. Even the clergymen praised me for having told the story, as if they were waiting for a non-Druze to do the job for them and finally tell their story, without fearing inside-communal penalties for discussing religious secrets. I was their Shabbes Goy [the gentile who carries out urgent errands for religious Jews on Saturdays, when work is prohibited]." One of the more respectable religious leaders, Sheikh Labib abu-Rukun, wrote the introductory note to the book.

One of Dana's most revealing studies deals with the delicate issue of intermarriage, offering a penetrating look into the dark alleys of the Druze community in Israel. In 1998 he launched a study, following some 150 cases of mixed marriages. The vast majority of all mixed marriages were of a Druze man marrying a non-Druze woman. Alas, none of the four women who were involved with non-Druze men is still alive. Eventually, a member of the family would execute the girl who dared wander in alien fields. A man who goes astray may be excommunicated. For a girl, that sanction is not strong enough. The death sentence will catch up with her, even if she moves to the end of earth.

Dana tells three stories that make the point in a chilling way. The first tells of a Druze woman who married a Christian Arab in 1948, converted to Christianity, and left the country for the U.S. to escape the wrath of her family. The family would not let go, however. They perceived her behavior as a disgrace to the family, the community, and the religion. The girl's brother traced the girl to her residence in America and knocked on her door, disguised as a beggar. When she opened the door, the brother pulled out a knife and stabbed her to death.

Some thirty years later, a Druze girl married a Christian in the village of Rameh, a mixed village of Druze, Christians, and Muslim Arabs. In that case, too, the family would not accept the non-Druze newcomer to the family. Several years later, that couple, too, was forced to leave the country. Once overseas, the couple felt safer and maintained regular contact with its family in Rameh. After several years abroad, they wanted to visit home, and family members gave their "word of honor" that no harm would come to them. Shortly after their arrival, however, the girl's soldier brother pulled out his rifle and killed her. "Family honor" was stronger than the "word of honor."

In the third case, in the early 1980s, Ibtihaj Hassoon of the village of Daliat al-Carmel married a Muslim, a member of the once-nomadic Bedouin community in a neighboring village.

The ancient fisherman's wharf of Acre.

The couple lived in peace for seventeen years in the Bedouin village, undisturbed by the girl's Druze family. One day, the woman's brother contacted her with appeasing, calming words. The brother supposedly had second thoughts about the family's turning its back to the daughter. Who am I, he said, to enforce my will on you? The brother proposed a *sulha*, the traditional peace pact between warring parties, which would lay bad feelings aside and would amount to an unconditional family pardon.

Alas, the woman took the bait, returned to her home village for the first time in seventeen years. As she was seen on the main street, her brother gunned her down in broad daylight. People stood by and applauded, said Dana. Family honor was saved once again.

"I remember searching for someone to condemn the mur-

der," recalled Dana, "but no one did." What is even more shocking is the notion that things have not changed. "Rebellious"
women are still subject to a family death warrant.

"To the best of my knowledge, this is just as bad today," said
Dana.

* * *

Intermarriages are banned as a means of avoiding assimilation. However, although the ban on intermarriage is absolute,
whether with Jews or with other Arabs, it appears to be more
effective in Israel than in the neighboring Arab countries.
Ultimately, the reason is greater tolerance for intermarriage
among Arabs than among Jews. The catch is that, even within a
purely Arab society, intermarriages harm Druze community
cohesiveness.

Dana served as military governor in Lebanon during the
Israeli occupation of 1982. "I felt that the Druze in Lebanon had
lost their Druze identity, precisely because intermarriages with
Muslims and Christian are so common. Although the Druze in
Lebanon are four times as numerous as in Israel, their Druze
consciousness is not as strong as in Israel." In other words, the
smaller the community, the stronger its communal bonds.
Sheikh Amin Tarif, the late legendary spiritual leader of the
community, once told Dana that the Druze identity in Israel is
stronger than it is among the Druze in both Syria and Lebanon.

Dr. Janan Falah noted in her book *The Druze Woman* that
Druze men in Syria and Lebanon can marry non-Druze
women, because the Druze community is registered as Muslim-
Druze. However, in the Golan Heights, which were annexed to
Israel, the religious establishment banned children born to
non-Druze mothers from joining Druze schools.

Dr. Janan Falah was born in the northern town of Acre, one of those rare cases in which a Druze was not born in a Druze village. Her father, Fares Falah, worked in Acre as a judge, the first Druze judge in Israel. She is now head of the Hebrew Literature Department at the Arab College in Haifa. She is married to a lawyer and accountant Iyyad Faraj. The couple has two children, a boy and a girl. It was not an easy match. It needed to cope with the bonds of tradition, and the way to cope was through patience, a heavy load of patience.

Iyyad courted Janan for years, and waited patiently for the father-judge to hand down his ruling. Would he agree to hand his precious daughter to the young law student? It was more or less a pre-sold game. The father knew he would eventually have to say "yes," but he took his time saying it. The young couple waited and waited and waited—until they got their way. Had Iyyad been a non-Druze, they would still be waiting; in fact, they probably would not have dated at all. The communal veto on intermarriages is much too strong.

It was a beautiful Saturday morning when we met Janan and her husband at the fishermen's wharf in the ancient town of Acre, sitting on the northern tip of the Haifa Bay. The colorful fishing boats were resting carelessly in the harbor after a hard night's work, while the blue sea was humming with speedboats and tourist boats. The ancient walls of the city and the human mixture of Arabs, Jews, and tourists added to the cosmopolitan air of the place. This is not the ideal place to preserve tribal values, we told Janan.

"Tell me about it," she said. "When my eldest was in kindergarten, he came home and told my mother and me he wanted to marry his girlfriend, a Russian immigrant. I laughed. But my mother said it was nothing to laugh about. You should educate him now that he'll only marry a Druze."

Janan's mother, from the perspective of age and experience, did not consider the incident a children's game, but rather an omen of the potential threats to the family's Druze identity many years later. "You must explain to him right now that we marry Druze only," advised the mother, and Janan obeyed. "Ever since that incident, I have told my kids time and again that we can be friends and neighbors with everyone, but we marry only Druze."

And Janan's son learned very early the facts of life: You have no choice but to turn down the romantic overtures of a young, attractive, blue-eyed, blonde, simply because she is a Russian immigrant, and you are a young proud Druze.

"How late do you let your fifteen-year-old son stay out at night?" we asked Janan.

"It's not just the time. He must tell us where he is. We check with the friends' parents. I won't let him go to pubs. He is too young. He can go to his friend's. We know the parents, and we keep in touch. Sometimes his father goes to bring him home, or I do, or he says he will come at a certain time. If not, we phone until he does."

The Druze in Israel gradually steered away from arranged marriages. Couples need the consent of their family to be engaged, but this is no longer dictated from above. Even among the Druze in the Golan Heights, however, arranged marriages are quite common. This was the theme of the film *The Syrian Bride,* an Israeli blockbuster production. The film recounts the story of Mona, a Druze bride in the Israeli occupied Golan Heights. She is engaged to be married with a Syrian television announcer in Damascus, across the border, whom she had never met before. Because the border between Israel and Syria is closed to the free movement of people, the wedding had to be held at the border. Mona's wedding day is the saddest day of her life, because once she crosses the border she is virtually cut off from her family in the Golan.

Mona nonetheless accepts her family's verdict. It is, indeed, in our eyes, a punishment. The girl must leave her family for a man she has never seen before (except on television), just so that family tradition can be honored. In Druze eyes, however, it may be less painful. Yes, the bride leaves her family for another, unknown, family across the border. Yet she remains with her people. Two families are drawn together by a sense of unity that transcends arbitrary borders. Whether there or here, they are at home.

One reason arranged marriages no longer work is attributed to co-education. Love flourishes in the classroom, and the parents can no longer enforce their choices upon the children. In the past, religious leaders punished parents who allowed their children to attend co-ed studies. Nowadays co-education is common. Despite the heavy burden of tradition, relations between boys and girls are much more liberal than in the previous generation. Boys and girls meet on mixed social occasions just like in any other Western society. They will not go on Western-style dates, but may meet secretly or go out escorted by an older member of the family. Premarital sex is considered taboo (though one that is sometimes violated).

However, what if a Druze girl wants to marry a Druze boy, contrary to the approval of her parents? The response of Professor Fadel Mansour, the scientist from Daliat al-Carmel, was loud and clear. "I told my daughters: I will not tell you whom to choose, but I will tell you who will not be acceptable. If you don't like my ruling, you can leave the family."

The bridegroom's father usually asks for the hand of the bride, and only then does the marriage process begin. Even so, the father will not go to the bride's parents before consulting first with his own family. The consent of the family is just as important as the consent of the couple.

Shehrezad Trabsheh is the daughter of Adnan, an actor and playwright who played, incidentally, a major role in *The Syrian Bride*. Although lovely Shehrezad, a pony-tailed attractive teenager, comes from a relatively modern, almost bohemian, progressive home, she, too, will accept the basic norms of Druze relationship between boys and girls. She will never court a boy; she will not even make eyes at him. "You can say yes or no, but you cannot pick your mate. If you fall in love, and the boy does not return your love, well, that's a disaster." Shehrezad was one of the teenagers we met at the Mughar youth center.

"We are taught to respect tradition from early age on," said Wa'ad Ghanem, Shehrezad's friend, wearing jeans and a T-shirt marked "Hollywood." "It pays. Unlike the Jews, we do not witness sexual molesting and mental abuse. We spend all our free time in the village; we go to the city only with our parents or some other adult. I like it this way, because I feel that I always have my guardian angel."

WEDDINGS

"YOU ARE SO BEAUTIFUL; WE will put you in a place of honor! We will cover you in jewelry and gold. We will cover you with roses, oh, beautiful bride!"

The elderly woman, standing among the crowd, at the foot of the bride's canopy, kept citing the wonders of the bride, chanting in a trilling, high-pitched voice, as if to make sure that everybody heard. Everyone heard. One could not escape this cry of joy, rolling from the top of this Galilean village of Beit Jann, all the way down the hill, to every street, every alley, every home.

For just a brief while, the bride became the queen of the village, and all villagers went out of their way to make her feel just that. A few days ahead of the wedding ceremony, a car with a loudspeaker drove around the village, inviting everyone to join the ceremony. Everyone, all ten thousand inhabitants were invited. Not everyone showed up, though. It is a self-selecting process. Those who are not welcome will not show up. Those who will show up are always welcome. And everyone knows whether one is welcome or not.

My crew and I were very fortunate to attend that wedding ceremony. Unlike some "modern" marriages, this wedding ceremony was strictly traditional. It was an opportunity to take a good look at a tradition that is losing its grip on Druze society. More often than not, young Druze couples get married in the same way their Jewish neighbors do—either at the parents'

Druze double wedding at Beit Jann.

home backyard or at a banquet hall. The "modern" ceremony is a one-time event, limited to three or four hours; a traditional ceremony, on the other hand, begins in the early afternoon, and continues into the evening. The parents of the bride will invite their relatives and friends to a rich dinner. The next evening, another dinner will be offered by the parents of the bridegroom.

The traditional wedding, however, is losing out to the changing winds of time. Just as young couples choose each other and no longer abide by arranged marriages, they also determine the nature of their wedding ceremony. The more traditional parents still insist that the bridegroom's father should visit the bride's father to ask for her hand, but that no longer happens in every case.

In the past, the process was so much more complex, and much more intriguing. The families were much more involved.

A young man who was interested in a woman sent her messages through his sister or a friend. Once he received a positive response, he would confide his intentions to his parents, who in turn asked for the young lady's parents' consent. Once the bride's parents agreed, an engagement ceremony took place. The young couple could then meet with each other, but not alone. The rule said that an elderly member of the family should be present to make sure that passion did not overcome modesty. That's the rule, though there are, of course, exceptions. Several months would pass between the engagement and the wedding. The wedding celebrations lasted several days. On the last day, the bride was brought to the groom's house, in a festive parade.

The wedding at Beit Jann involved three families, because it was actually a double wedding. Brothers Shahin and Rafa' Shahin were marrying Lina Sa'ad and Jihan Keis, all of the same village. In the past, the ideal situation—in the eyes of the parents, that is—was a "Badal" marriage. In a Badal marriage, two brothers marry simultaneously two sisters, or a brother and a sister marry a brother and a sister of another family.

This was a perfect arrangement for the parents: two for the price of one. However, more often than not, this would turn out to be an unfortunate match for at least one of the four people concerned. Moreover, such a marriage is interconnected for life. Not only is it an enforced marriage, but marital problems with one couple may also lead to a collapse of the marriage of the other couple because of ill feelings among the families concerned. If, God forbid, one couple decides to separate, the other couple must separate as well. This makes the separation process even more complex than usual, often resulting in no action, with the two couples stuck with each other for the rest of their lives. Such Badal marriages have become less and less common.

Nonetheless, the wedding that we attended had a certain flavor of that traditional marital transaction. We were standing in the crowd, among Jihan's family, at the family's garage, waiting for the ceremony to begin. The bride, dressed in her traditional white dress, covered with shekel and dollar bills—"symbolic" gifts attached to her dress—was sitting on a canopy, waiting to be driven to her new home, unable to control her tears. Her mother stood crying beside her. Almost every woman was crying. They cried as if Jihan was crossing the border into Syria, although Jihan and Rafa' would continue to live in the same village. One by one, the women bid farewell to the young woman, knowing that today would be her last day at home, as *her* home. From now on, she would only come as a visitor. I pulled out a handkerchief, getting ready. Once everyone started crying, I knew I would start to cry, too.

The wedding ceremony is the climax of a long preparation process. Prior to the wedding ceremony (no specific time span, a few days or even months or years), the young couple meets for the *aqd* ceremony, the Druze version of the *ktuba,* in the presence of the parents, to sign the accord of marriage before an imam, the officiating Druze priest. The signed agreement goes to the religious court for ratification, but once the *aqd* is signed, they are man and wife, with reservations. No sexual relations before the actual wedding, the *jawaz* ceremony, but they would need to be officially divorced for the marriage to be annulled.

Wedding customs have adopted past tribal practice, when the bride moved from her own tribe to the tribe of the bridegroom, thus giving up all her past belongings. It was now the bridegroom's duty to compensate her for her material loss. The father of the bridegroom brings dowry to the family of the bride. This is actually a formal symbolic act, since eventually the bride's parents return the gift. Now, in Beit Jann, all pre-marital arrangements had been taken care of, the new houses were ready, the doors were open for a new life.

The wedding ceremony began with lunch. The Shahin family placed a huge tent in the backyard of their home, a cover for a multitude of long tables loaded with food and seating hundreds of guests. Everything went very fast. Guests—men only—stood in line to be greeted by the bridegrooms, their father, brothers, uncles, and village elders. The menu was standard: salads, humus, mutton, chicken, rice, and, on a separate table, fruits and sweets. Members of the family—men only—served as waiters, rushing from the kitchen to keep filling the platters.

Wedding meals are less of a social gathering than a gorging ceremony. People don't sit back on full stomachs to relax and chat. They finish eating and vacate their seats to allow another round of guests to enjoy the food.

Once the meal was over, the guests lined up again to bid farewell and hand the family envelopes and checks. Whereas in a Jewish ceremony any gift below the value of $50 is considered a disgrace, Druze religious leaders have suggested that gifts should be modest, sometimes as little as $10, so as not to insult those who cannot give very much. In any case, monetary gifts are considered a good investment. Everyone knows that the more wedding gifts one makes, the more likely one will receive many times over that amount when it comes to wedding ceremonies in one's own family.

After the festive lunch, it was time for a break. Both brides and bridegrooms sat at the houses of their parents. The bridegrooms sat in their parents' living room, watching TV, surrounded by friends and looking as if they didn't know what hit them, hoping for the best.

Finally, around 4 P.M. a delegation of the bridegroom's family came to the bride's residence. The delegates stood in one long line on the street, facing a delegation of the bride's family across the street. For a while they just stood there, facing each other, with relatives of the bride passing with trays full of goodies, sweets and fruit, and light drinks. Both parties acted as if they did not know the purpose of the respected delegation, waiting for the guests to make the first move. A representative of the bridegroom's delegation suggested that one of the elders speak on behalf of the bridegroom's family, asking for the family's permission to let the bride go. The person performing the act should be one of the more respected persons in the community. Thus, for several moments they kept passing the honor from one elder to another, very much like Barak and Arafat did, suggesting that the other be the first to enter the Camp David negotiations hut. Eventually one respected member of the delegation consented. He faced the bride's delegation and formally asked for the hand of Jihan. Jihan's family delegation answered in chorus, "Yes, permission is given."

It was now time for the bride to leave the podium, escorted by an uncle. Her face was covered with the bridal veil and a cloak, an *abaya* ("so that she can no longer tell the way back"), and she slowly made her way to the car amid weeping and occasional cries of joy by one of the village's elderly women.

The bridal car rolled slowly down the hill, through the narrow alleys of the village toward the residence of the brothers, followed by a motorcade of the bride's relatives. The drivers refrained from honking, taking consideration of a family in the village that sat in mourning. The bride's parents did not escort her to her new home. They had just bid farewell to their daughter. Next time they would meet with their daughter would be later that afternoon, as guests at the residence of the bridegroom's family.

Throughout the wedding ceremony no music was played, no songs, no dancing. "Religion does not object to music as such," explained Sheikh Samih Natour of Daliat al-Carmel, "but rather against the use of music for mixed dancing." Druze religious law does permit music in ceremonies attended separately by men and women.

The bridal motorcade arrived. The cars of both brides stopped in front of the Shahin residence. The brides came out of the car and posed for a family photo—the two couples with the bridegrooms' mother in between. Once the bride arrived at her new home, she received a *hamireh* (a piece of dough), in which she placed coins and flowers. Now each couple glued the dough onto the house well as a sign of wealth and happiness.

As evening fell, the guests gradually dispersed. It was now time for the young couples to mount their bridal bed and spend their first night together. Surprisingly, unlike other religions, which make a point of preparing the young couple (especially the bride) for the big night, young Druze women get no authoritative premarital advice. They will often learn the complex facts of life from their parents, but sometimes the parents are too shy to cope with the challenge. A couple will thus need to consult with other family relatives, with a doctor, or with a social worker—or else they will need to explore the new paths of love on their own. Many do, in fact, and find the task quite enjoyable.

The new home is not just any new home. It was the bridegroom's entry ticket to marriage. The bride's parents will run an economic checkup to make sure that the bridegroom can meet the challenge. The bridegroom, with the help of his family, needs to exploit the time between the engagement and the wedding to build the house, so that the young couple can spend the wedding night at their new home. This is a cruel custom.

Often young men who cannot afford to build a home must postpone their marriages.

The ambitious "Israeli Society" web project, produced at Haifa University and edited by Professor Oz Almog and Dr. Tamar Almog, notes in its lengthy description of the Druze home, that in such cases often the wedding will either be postponed, or the young couple will need to inhabit an uncompleted house.

Also, because of rising construction costs, the bridegroom's family often takes care of the initial cost only, leaving the rest to be shared with the bride's family and the mortgage to the young couple. This is why it is customary to marry within a certain socioeconomic class to share the burden.

Although most Druze are no longer farmers, they nevertheless cling to the traditional rural housing style: a one-floor villa with a large garden. This is yet another reason for the rising construction cost, explain the Almogs in their project. This creates greater congestion in the village, but it also leads to expansion of the village and its beauty.

Many houses stand on top of poles, creating a closed space for an additional apartment for the children in the future, as well as avoiding moisture in the present. At times the bottom floor will be used to build a housing unit for an elderly parent who can no longer live independently—yet another example of the Druze tradition of mutual aid. Unlike the Jewish social environment, the Druze—and for that matter all Arabs—will not abandon their parents at an old age home, regardless of their condition. One of the children will always take care of the parent in need.

On top of almost every house stands a water container. It's not that there isn't running water, but rather a remnant of the old days, when outside water sources were not secure. Although the public supply of water is secure today, many Druze homes continue to pump water from a backyard well, also a remnant of the past. Water from a private well, they believe, is cleaner, safer, and tastier than water from the Mekorot national water company.

The standard dwelling in a Druze village comprises three bedrooms and a spacious living room. In accordance with the Druze custom of generous hospitality, the living room is not just the main family room. It is particularly spacious, to accommodate as many guests as possible. The entire entrance floor at the Birani residence in Daliat al-Carmel is actually the *diwan,* the traditional Arabic name for a living room. It is a complex of a spacious rectangular room, which can accommodate dozens of guests, an adjacent smaller dining room and two other rooms. The walls are covered with photos, telling the life story of the master of the house, Ali Birani, showing him side by side with historic celebrities such as King Hussein of Jordan, Israel's slain Prime Minister Yitzhak Rabin, and film star Richard Gere, who was a personal guest at the residence. The guest book dates back to the early 1960s, with signatures of one Valéry Giscard d'Estaing, who later became president of France, and an Egyptian VIP who signed "a friend from Egypt," to avoid fundamentalist criticism at home for his contact with the "Zionist" Druze.

Family quarters are separated, at a lower floor, with three bedrooms surrounding the huge kitchen and family dining room, obviously the core of the residence.

Some traditional diwans are comprised of colorfully decorated mattresses and pillows lying on the floor, a sitting corner used by guests to rest after a rich meal, or by religious persons who refrain from sitting on chairs.

One of the customary decorations for a typical living room

is the Druze flag, which is made up of five colors: green, red, yellow, blue, and white. Green stands for "the mind," *'al-'akl*, to better understand the truth; red is for "the soul," *'an-nafs*; yellow stands for "the word," *'al-kalima*, the purest form of expression of the truth; blue stands for the mental power of the will, *'as-sabik*, and white, the realization of the mental power in the material world, *'al-tali*.

Other customary decorations are "The Blue Eye," a protection from the evil eye; a verse from the Koran, the Druze Holy Scriptures; and pictures of family members, along with various dignitaries to emphasize their social value; pictures of community dignitaries, such as the deceased spiritual leader Sheikh Amin Tarif; and photos of holy places, such as the site of Nabi Shueib, the burial place of Prophet Jethro, the most important Druze prophet.

There is always strict separations between the parents' section, the boys' room, and the girls' room. The children's rooms, in sharp contrast with the other rooms in the house, are decorated with posters of rock and sport stars—a vivid manifestation of the giant leap from a traditional into a Western-oriented society. Children usually stay at home until they get married. And if they don't get married, they rarely leave the house and live on their own.

THE DRUZE WOMAN

JUDGING BY THE ROW OF buses stopping in front of the shop, one would think that the country was suffering an acute shortage of soap. One bus follows another, unloading bargain hunters straight into the soap shop of Savta Jamila. The shoppers surround the colorful soap stands, and fill their bags with a multitude of bars, as if Savta Jamila's "Wonder Soap" can actually scrub off all aches, pains, sins and other misfortune.

Although Jamila Hiar is a proud Druze woman, she named the brand of her homemade olive-soap "Savta Jamila," or grandma Jamila in Hebrew. Savta Jamila sells better in Hebrew. She is the boss of the small family business. Despite only two years of formal education, she invented what she claims to be "the best soap in the world." She developed the formula of the soap, she manufactures it, she runs the shop, and she is in charge of public relations. We cannot judge how good the soap is, but her PR is superb.

The New Middle East is still quite shaky, but there certainly *is* a New Woman in the Middle East, and her name is Savta Jamila. Although she, too, wears the traditional *futa*, the white head kerchief, she has disassociated herself from the traditional role of the Arab woman as a secondary to her husband. She has become the envy of many liberated women. She cooks the food and concocts the soap; she spoils the grandchildren and runs downstairs to indoctrinate yet another group of customers who want to hear all about the wonders of the soap; and she hands out coffee and watches the cash register ... closely.

Her shop, workshop, and residence are all in one building, which stands at the entrance to the ancient village of Peki'in and has a breathtaking view of the Galilee Mountains. On display in the shop are framed letters with testimonials that Savta Jamila's Wonder Soap cures skin ailments, acne, psoriasis, dandruff, baldness, hemorrhoids, you name it. Wonder Soap smells good, cleans thoroughly, and best of all—makes terrific sales. All thanks to her "secret" formula of pure olive oil and a variety of herbs, straight from the mountains of Galilee.

The reason Jamila has almost no formal education is that her parents forced her to leave school after second grade to help support the family. "I used to ride my donkey for hours on end to work in the fields," she recalls. It was then, as a child, that she became acquainted with the various herbs and their therapeutic virtues. It was then that she became intimate with the fields and spoke to the herbs—and they responded.

She married at sixteen and by seventeen gave birth to her first son. Many women began their adult life at the same age, spending their lives between the kitchen, the children, and the husband. But Jamila was determined to make a difference. For years she didn't mind being illiterate; you don't need to read and write to work in the fields or to make soap, she said. However, when Fuad, her eldest, returned home from school and she was unable to help him with his homework, she knew she had to do something about it.

She began studying through Na'amat, the women's organization of the country's giant labor union, the Histadrut. After years of studies, she could read, write, and master the math needed to run a business. Na'amat quickly became Jamila's work place. First she was a coordinator with the Arab women in the regions, then she became Na'amat's director of vocational training.

During her free time (which was usually late at night), she began experimenting with various formulae to manufacture her natural health, wonder soap. She was often busier with her soaps than with her children. "Both of us were uneducated," recalled Kamal, Jamila's husband. Income was low, and the young family could barely make ends meet. They had watched with envy how friends and neighbors were prospering. "I told my wife, 'As far as I am concerned, you can do whatever you like.' She believed in the soap business, and I didn't stand in her way. I was ready to open for her every possible door, to get every possible loan, even if that meant selling our house to the neighbors."

"I remember begging my mother for shoes, but there was no money," said Fuad. "She used to take the leftovers of cooking oil, trying to manufacture soap. Sometimes we watched her working with tears in our eyes. Frankly, we thought she was crazy. There is more to life than soap. But we accepted her folly as it was, because in our society we grow up respecting our parents. We children were also recruited into the business. My mother used to send me on a donkey loaded with water tanks to plant olive trees. I did so obediently. She told me, when you grow up, you will understand. Only now do I begin to understand what mother did for us."

Jamila began concocting the soap at home, "just for the heck of it," crystallizing it and cutting it into pieces. It was a process of trial and error. "I experienced long years of failure before I hit the right formula," she recalls. "I used to try all kinds of herbs and didn't tell anyone what I was doing. When a person experiments and fails, people say he is foolish, and when he succeeds, they try to trip him. I worked quietly; I used to hand out my soap for free, and wait for feedback, until I was sure that I hit it right."

She then placed her soaps for sale in a small shop in the front of the house. Local and foreign visitors, hungry for exotic deals, liked the woman who offered the magic of the olive tree for sale.

"A lady from Switzerland had cut her finger, and the scar would not heal," recalled Fuad, now the business's executive vice president for marketing. "The Swiss hospital gave up on the lady and suggested that she try a curing session at the Dead Sea. On the way to the Dead Sea, she met an Israeli lawyer who suggested that she try the soap. He melted the soap in a microwave, spread the ointment on the scar, and wrapped it with a bandage. The scar disappeared after five days."

As the stories about the wonders of the soap spread, the small workshop expanded, and the boys offered a helping hand. Imad became plant manager, and Farres shared the secret formulae with his mother.

A souvenir shop across the street tried to compete, but failed. No one cracked the secrets of the soap; no one matched the business leadership of Jamila.

In 2004, Jamila opened a new workshop—and a new sales shop—at the Tefen industrial park, part of a local complex of museums. Jamila now employs twenty-five workers, selling thirty thousand to forty thousand bars a month, for an average of $4 a bar, with sales exceeding $1.5 million a year. In May 2006, she was one of twelve citizens chosen to light a torch in a state ceremony on Mt. Herzl in Jerusalem, marking the beginning of Independence Day festivities.

Fuad, a reserve officer in the Israeli army, the first Druze graduate of the military academy, now reaches out overseas, opening Savta Jamila branches in Amsterdam and New York.

Their brand name is "Gamila Healing Soap." They spell the name "Gamila" but say "Jamila," Arabic for "the beautiful one." The business runs a web page, www.gamilasoap.com. It boasts that the "legendary Gamila" can neither read nor write. Not true, but that story sells better.

Fuad did not join the business until 2003. By the age of forty-six he had tried quite a number of business ventures, not all of them successful. He was the first Druze to graduate from the military academy. When he quit the army as a captain in reserves, he made a living for several years working as a security officer for a number of organizations, mostly in Amsterdam.

"One day, as I sat in a coffee house in Amsterdam, someone told me that he was suffering from melanoma. I immediately thought of my mother's soap. 'Try the soap,' I told him. 'If it doesn't help, it won't hurt.' One month later, my mother came to Holland. By that time I forgot all about the melanoma guy. Just as she was staying with us, he called me up that he wanted to come and visit. When he saw mother, he just couldn't stop praising her. As far as he was concerned, the soap had cured the cancerous illness. 'Look,' he said, pointing at his arms, 'I have the skin of a baby!'

"I don't know whether it was the soap that was the magic cure, or whether the guy had not really suffered from melanoma, but, in any case, I decided that this is too serious a business to stay away from, and I returned home."

As we are talking, a group of shoppers arrives. They ask Jamila to give them a lecture about the soap, but Jamila is busy serving us lunch. She apologizes, takes time out to meet with the customers and tell them all about the soap. She returns in half an hour, complaining: "That's the story of my life, I was hoping to sit down with you and enjoy your company, but they keep me busy all the time. I am like a soldier on duty from sunrise to sunset."

Fuad now plans to open a chain of soap shops throughout America. "I am not selling soap, but rather a brand name. People will buy it because it's the best soap in the world."

As the business turns into an empire, Savta Jamila is its empress. A giant leap and quite rare in the Middle Eastern, male-dominated society. "Let's face it," said Fuad, "had it not been for our encounter with the Jews, we would have still been shepherds in the mountains." And Jamila would still be picking herbs.

Unlike the general custom in Arab society, Jamila's husband Kamal is proud of depending on his wife. The Druze religious leader Amir Abdullah a-Tanuki decreed 500 years ago that women and men should be equal in life and religion; the man should teach his wife the worship of God, he should teach her to read and write, and if he is unable to do so, he should provide her with a teacher.

Jamila is Kamal's only wife, however. Even in today's Middle East, it is quite common among Muslims to marry a second wife. After all, Islam permits marrying as many as four wives, as long as the husband is capable of taking care of all their needs—*all* their needs, that is. This is not the case for the Druze. A basic rule of Druze religion bans a man from marrying a second wife. His must have only one wife, who must also be Druze, otherwise he is excommunicated by the community—a harsh sanction. He can no longer live in the village, he is not entitled to any inheritance, and none of his children can marry within the community.

Jamila was a rebel. She dared to go against the religious establishment. Despite religious bans, she was one of the first Druze women in the village to join her husband in working

Bakery in a Druze village.

outside of the village. Although Druze religion does not discriminate between men and women, the clergy like to see the women kept at home and controlled by the men. In the past, girls were forbidden, by order of the village religious elders, from leaving the village to study. At times they were even excommunicated for getting an education, along with their families—the worst possible sanction in Druze society.

Because of the religious ban on girls' education, for many years, Druze girls stayed at home, uneducated. Not anymore. Today hundreds of Druze women study in institutes of higher learning away from the village. The community boasts several women lawyers and engineers and three physicians. Some eighty-four percent of Druze students are women; ten are medical students.

The first Ph.D (other than in medicine) was awarded to Dr.

Janan Farraj-Falah, an expert in Hebrew literature and the author of *The Druze Woman*, which was invaluable in helping us understand the role of women in today's Druze society. Janan, like Jamila, openly criticizes the role of religious leaders in keeping the Druze society (particularly the Druze woman) backward. Hers is an exceptional book, because it takes courage to come out against the religious establishment of this still-traditional society.

Janan drives a brand-new VW Beetle, ignoring the religious traditional ban on women drivers. Yes, that's right—Druze clergy ban women from driving. They are so concerned for the reputation of the women that they want to prevent them from driving outside the control of their husbands and families. To protect them from non-Druze men, or any other outside dangers, women are limited in their movement. If the wind blows through an open window, the window should be shut, said Professor Fadel Mansour. "God forbid she has a flat tire at night; what then?" asked Mansour. At times the clergy may use sanctions against women drivers or even against their passengers. Most nonreligious women disregard the ban and ignore such sanctions, which has been a source of tension between the religious and the secular segments in the society.

Although Professor Mansour understands the logic behind the ban on driving, he, too, agreed that the ban against women driving was redundant. "Although I, too, prefer that women should not drive, I am one of the few clergymen who do object to an absolute ban on driving."

In her book, Janan outlines the basic rights of the Druze women, quoting great Druze sages. Some of them conflict with the customary rulings of contemporary clergy: There is no religious ban on women attending wedding parties with music and dances. Religion encourages women to study. Religion compels the man to respect his wife and, when necessary, hire "a teacher and a maid" to help her. Hamza bin Ali, one of the first propagators of the Druze religion, decreed that "the Druze (man) must make his wife equal to himself for all intents and purposes."

No girl can be forced to marry against her will, or to be married under the age of fifteen. Religion allows the use of contraception. Abortion is permitted, because the fetus is not considered a human being. "As long as the fetus is inside the womb, it has no soul, and therefore abortion is permitted," said Dr. Falah.

Religion bans polygamy, but the society shows greater tolerance toward a man who betrays his wife than the other way round. An unfaithful wife may pay for her "sins" with her life. An unfaithful husband may, at worst, be excommunicated by the religious circles. Moreover, despite an absolute religious ban on murder, the so-called honor killing of women may also take place in the Druze society.

Druze religion allows for family planning. If you are poor, you may even have only one child. The usual custom is to allow a time span of five years between one birth and another, allowing two years for breast-feeding.

Unlike Islam, there is no forced divorce. The woman can divorce her husband, which is not possible among Muslims. Divorce is irreversible, subject to the agreement of both parties. A divorced couple cannot remarry. This measure is taken to prevent harsh divorces and illegitimate pressure on a divorcee to return to the spouse. Some couples, however, have found a way to circumvent this ban. Both husband and wife converted to Islam, and were remarried by a Muslim qadi (religious judge). This, the Druze community was willing to accept, realizing the conversion was not for real.

Not only is a divorcee banned from remarrying her husband, it is also inadvisable that she remarry anyone at all. The reason, said Professor Fadel Mansour, is the welfare of the children. They should not be exposed to a "new" father while their real father is still alive. Rather cruel, isn't it? Perhaps, said Mansour, but that's fate. The welfare of the children takes precedence over their mother's.

Widows are, so to speak, "better off." They do get a second chance. Aliza, the wife of fallen soldier Lutfi Nasser a-Din who was gunned down by Palestinian terrorists in the Arava, remarried. She wed Jihad, her late husband's uncle and the younger brother of her father-in-law, Amal Nasser a-Din. "It was important for me that she remarry within the family," said Amal Nasser a-Din. "I was concerned that if she marries someone else, my son's children would be detached from the family."

Druze women have made tremendous progress in recent years. Not only are girls the majority among Druze students, also their fertility rate is dropping fast from the 7.9 per thousand in the fifties to a current figure of less than two per thousand. The Druze woman is no longer perceived solely as a wife and a mother. Religious practices have granted the Druze woman a fair amount of independence and freedom. Druze women are free to make their own decisions and to determine their own fate. The woman is entitled, for example, to issue her own will.

This is all very nice on paper, but in practice Druze women often have to comply with the dictates of the men in the family. Although women are considered equal and are more easily accepted to the *uqel*, or religious circles, the religious establishment as such is dominated by men. Only men determine whether one meets the conditions to join the religious circle; only men issue sanctions against violations of the religious code. The hardest punishment, of course, is the *muqata'a,* or excommunication from the community. Although the woman is equal, there are certain functions that are considered beyond limits for women. This is part of a tradition influenced by the Arab patriarchal society and may at times conflict with the Druze religion. The woman should not expose her body, and she cannot be a warrior or a farmer because of her role as a mother.

Professor Mansour totally endorses this approach. "I am against raping nature. The world was introduced to corruption on the day that women began wearing trousers," said the scientist.

TRADITION AND SECULARISM

WITHIN A FIVE-MINUTE WALK FROM the home of Professor Mansour, almost across the street, lives another Mansour family, Najwa and Ghassan Mansour. Even if we take the professor's comments with a grain of salt, this couple is the ultimate manifestation how far those comments are from present-day reality. Here is a family in which both husband and wife share the trousers. They believe in modernism, in open education, and behave like any other middle-class family in the Western hemisphere—and yet, at the same time, maintain the bonds to Druze tradition.

Wide stairs lead down from the street to the spacious house, characterized by wide glass doors and windows—an architectural expression of Druze hospitality. The private rooms of family members are hidden away from the public eye, but the front radiates openness and an invitation to come in and relax. The living room overlooks the green slopes of Mt. Carmel and the Gulf of Haifa.

Najwa teaches English at the local high school. Her husband Ghassan is a certified public accountant. Eleven-year-old Yarin is a junior-high school student and wants to be a lawyer or an architect. Her older brother Ayal, sixteen, studies in the tenth grade. He's an enthusiastic basketball player who spends at least one night a week as a volunteer in the village civil guard and earns his pocket money working as a counselor at a local summer camp.

In the past, Ayal went to a Jewish high school in Haifa, with the idea that graduating from a Hebrew school would in the future make university studies easier. However, the challenge was much too burdensome. Ayal, who used to be the natural class leader at his junior high in the village, suddenly became the alien outsider, the village boy who came to study in the city and could not quite master the dominant language, Hebrew. Ayal could not adjust to becoming a back-row student. He preferred to be at the head of his peers rather than a tail to the Jewish students. At his home school, he feels more appreciated, a feeling that many Druze carry with them throughout their lives.

It's a short ride from the Mansour family's Druze village to the big Jewish city. For Ayal Mansour and his friends, it's a journey of contrasts. When Ayal and his friends go down to Haifa, they are not quite at ease. It is not *their* mall that they visit, but their neighbors' mall. The big city is tempting. The young Druze boys window-shop, go to the movies, watch the girls go by. Watch, do not touch, say the parents.

"We just have some fun," said Ayal. "We go out and drink something—nonalcoholic, of course—go to the mall, buy things, you know."

Despite the family's modern appearance, the parents draw a strict line that should distinguish them from their Jewish friends. If anything, Najwa laments that the line is not strict enough. "We deal too little with education. We are trying too hard to be our son's friends, and we forget our role as parents. We educate them by being a role model for them," said Najwa. "Though I know that no child wants to ever be like his parents, once they grow up they come back, yes, exactly like their parents."

As much as Najwa Mansour is a progressive woman who has been exposed to the secrets of the wide world, there are some borders she would never cross. "I will never wear either a bathing suit or a miniskirt or shorts. Neither here, nor abroad. You never leave your values behind; you take them with you, anywhere."

This constant conflict between the need to preserve traditional values and outside temptations is the cause of many sleepless nights for Druze parents. They, too, face the dilemmas, not just their children.

"I educate my children with respect and love," said Fuad Hiar, the son of Grandma Jamila, the soap empress from Peki'in. "But at the same time I draw very strict lines—foremost among them, absolute respect for the family."

In his appearance, Fuad is the total opposite of his mother. Whereas grandma Jamila always wears her traditional headscarf and long skirt, Fuad's appearance is completely Western. At the age of forty-eight, he is stylishly bold, shaving his head not for religious reasons but because it looks better on him. ("I never use shaving cream, only Jamila's soap.") He wears fashionable jeans and brand-name shirts and speaks fluent Hebrew, often mixed with English expressions, as if to make the point stronger. Traveling often between Tel-Aviv and Amsterdam for the family's soap business, he has become a member of the new Israeli jet set.

Nevertheless, even Fuad, a man of the world, is concerned that his children will be drugged with an overdose of freedom. "Just as democracy has its limits, so should the liberal education of our children. I feel that career-oriented Western parents often invest less in the children and in their education, all under the pretext of freedom and democracy.

"We Westerners give our children too much freedom, and I am afraid that we Druze are also infected with it. One of the lessons I would like to draw from our tradition is to know how to slap or spank a child in the right place, at the right time. Believe me, it isn't easy. Often, when I slap my child, I am the one who goes up to my room and cries. It hurts me, but later, when I think about it, I know that this slap had a moderating influence on the child. The slap helps the child to recognize the framework, to make sure that there are no boundaries broken. A child who is not educated properly loses respect for the parents."

It's easy for him to say such things. As a teenager Fuad himself enjoyed his share of "excess" freedom. He was the first Druze to study in the army's IDF Junior Command Preparatory School in Haifa, with no parents to boss him around. The school is located amid a posh neighborhood on Mt. Carmel, within walking distance from city entertainment centers. In addition to military studies, civilian studies take place at the nearby, highly prestigious Re'ali School, which is a co-ed institution.

For young Fuad, this was a giant leap from the traditional rural environment of Peki'in to the very Western, open society of Haifa. Regardless of his upbringing and his traditional values, he was exposed to the Jewish, Western way of life. He would need quite a measure of self-discipline not to succumb to temptation.

"Indeed, when I lived in Haifa, I underwent a crisis of identity. I was different from the others; I was Druze, and they were Jewish. At the same time, I wanted to become one of them." Fuad's formula to solve that identity crisis was to win the respect of his friends as a Druze. He won their respect by using the carrot and stick technique. He indoctrinated his friends with the knowledge that there was nothing a Druze would not do to gain honor and respect. "They knew that I could kill if they disrespected me." With the help of his muscular appearance, the message got through. Rarely did anyone challenge him.

The carrot part of the deal was winning his friends' hearts with "corruption meals" and drinks on the house. Whereas most of his Jewish friends came from well-to-do homes and seldom suffered from shortages of cash, Fuad's family was relatively poor at the time. "I used to work once or twice a month as a guard or a docker in the harbor, making some NIS 2,000 a month—most of which I used to spend on our parties at school. I felt rich."

After Fuad Hiar ended his military service, he served as a security officer in Holland, where, as things go, he met a pretty Dutch girl and fell head over heels for her. "The temptations are huge," recalled Fuad. "You grow up in a Western society and study with people from around the world, and you develop friendships." Fuad was about to marry his Dutch girlfriend when Fuad's mother Jamila intervened.

"I said to him: 'You are a big boy. I can't tell you what to do. I can only advise you: If you love this girl enough to give up on having a mother, father, and family, then go and be well. But it will be as if I had four sons and now I have three.' " No one wants to lose one's family, one's mom, one's dad, and one's brothers and sisters. It is a family disgrace that few Druze would dare to face, even for the love of their life. Fuad gave in and gave up on his love. He returned home to mother, to the family, and eventually got married to a Druze girl.

"I was overjoyed," recalled Jamila. "On the day he married, I was the happiest woman in the world, because I didn't lose my son."

Fuad is not religious. In defiance of religious laws, he often shares a glass of wine with his son. On the other hand, he will never drink alcohol in public. "It is not what you do, but how you do it."

Fuad graduated from the military school in 1979 and became an officer in the prestigious IDF Golani Brigade. He served several years as a career officer, left the army in 1986 with the rank of captain, and tried a variety of jobs. After his marriage in 1997, the family moved to Holland for an initial exploration of the overseas soap market.

In Holland, it was his son Amir, twelve years old, who needed to cope with the local temptations, this time those of the Dutch society. Suddenly it was Fuad's challenge to draw the line for his children. For once, he was pleased with the results. One day, the family planned to go to the beach. "The neighbor's son wanted to join us, but his father said no. The boy protested rudely, yelling and screaming. My son, rather than identifying with his friend, was in shock at his friend's disrespect for his parents."

The challenges and conflicts continued once the family returned to Israel. Contrary to Druze customs, Fuad decided to build his home away from his family and the village. The young family moved to Kfar Veradim, a high-quality, expensive dwelling outside the town of Ma'elot, a fifteen-minute drive from his home village of Peki'in. The children are still young; Amir is twelve, his sister Yasmin is seven, and Noor Daniel is a newborn.

"Friends ask me, 'How can you expose your children to alien Jewish culture?' My answer is simple: My son in the Jewish village, or even in Holland, is more Druze than my brother's son who lives in the Druze village. A boy raised in the village is not expected to identify with being a Druze; being Druze is obvious. My son, on the other hand, needs to tell himself every day anew that he is Druze. Thus, in a way, he is a much more conscientious Druze than his cousin in the village.

"Children of friends of mine who moved with their parents to the southern town of Eilat have forgotten their Arabic and speak only Hebrew. But my children speak Arabic along with Hebrew, Dutch, and English.

"Often in class, Amir tells his classmates about the Druze, their customs and way of life. I remember how, back in school in Holland, the Dutch teacher once devoted a lesson to the story of the Creation according to various religions. He got up and asked, 'How come you don't speak about the Druze version of the Creation?' The teacher admitted she knew nothing about it and asked Amir to talk about it. So he stood there, only seven years old and gave them a lecture about the Druze, about their history, their belief in reincarnation, and posed a question: 'If God is indeed almighty, why do the Jews believe that he needed to rest on Saturday?'"

Fuad is different from the average Druze. He dares challenge the customs and the *bon ton* of Druze society. "You must understand. I am not the typical Druze. Most of my adult life I lived outside the village. I cherish my privacy and individualism, which are not easy to preserve in the village. When you live in the village, you waste a lot of time and energy on redundant social commitments such as gossip, discussion of the latest wedding, or your aunt's previous life according to Druze belief in reincarnation. My son, too, when he comes to the village and hears religious or political radicals, he sees things that he doesn't like; it is not the village he had envisaged."

Although Fuad honored his mother's wish and gave up his plans to marry a Dutch girl, now when his oldest son is only twelve years old he declares that he will never repeat his mother's behavior. "I don't know how I will cope with the challenges, but I know one thing: Unlike my mother, I will always stand behind my children, regardless of their choice of lifestyle.

"At this stage in his life, Amir is convinced that he will marry a Druze. When we lived in Holland, a Dutch girl once told him she wanted to marry him. Amir, hardly seven years old, said, 'No way.' The girl insisted: 'I will become Druze, too.' But he explained to her that it was impossible."

At Kfar Veradim, the children's friends are Jewish, the school is Jewish, and the temptations are Jewish. How will Amir preserve his Druze heritage in three or four years, when he is part of the Jewish teenage society? Fuad may be confident in the strength of Druze heritage, but he, too, knows that the challenge will be big. "Frankly, the challenge is already there, in front of my very eyes. My son tells me that the class party begins at 10:30 p.m.; so if that's when it starts, then when does it end? It is rather difficult for me to adjust to the changing times, and I know it will become harder and harder as the years go by. I try to educate my children to cope with the world of twenty or thirty years from now, when I am no longer there to tell them around the clock what's right and what's wrong."

What makes the continuous encounter with tradition particularly rewarding is the fact that it is usually associated with food—good food.

Evening fell on Nabi Shueib, the holiest site for the Druze, when the Birani family gathered to celebrate the implementation of a vow. The women struggled with resolve against the stubborn mountain breeze that threatened to blow away the white paper cloth covering the long table. Their mission was to cover the wooden table with a rich assortment of salads as the men were busy grilling the lamb chops. The children were playing in the garden adjacent to the large parking lot leading to the holy site. Farther up the hill, in a hidden hall inside this huge building, stands the tomb of Prophet Shueib, or the Biblical Jethro, the most important prophet in Druze tradition.

The Druze have set April 25 as the annual date for the *ziara*, the annual pilgrimage to the site, which continues for four days of festivities, rallies, prayers, and social and family gatherings. However, it was a regular Friday evening in the middle of August when the Birani family in full force—Grandpa Ali, six children, and ten grandchildren—gathered at the site, along with a number of other Druze families.

The tomb is located in the ancient site of the Horns of Hittin, west of Tiberias, overlooking Lake Kinneret (Sea of Galilee). This is where Muslim warrior Saladin overcame the Crusaders in a turning-point battle on July 4, 1187. The exhausted and thirst-crazed Crusader army was largely annihilated, opening the way for Saladin, who headed south to conquer Jerusalem.

According to Druze tradition, Saladin had a dream on the eve of that battle in which an angel had promised him victory if, after the battle, he would gallop westward on his horse. Wherever the stallion would pull up, the angel promised, he would find the burial site of Nabi Shueib. When the dream came true, the Druze built a tomb at the site, next to which is a rock bearing a footprint believed to be that of Nabi Shueib himself.

At Nabi Shueib, centuries-old traditions meet with everyday life. Not only is the site a place of pilgrimage and worship, it is also a place for communal meetings and for family celebrations.

At the age of two, Ali's grandson Ayal refused to speak. He felt at peace with his baby talk, and would not make any progress. The parents, Ali's son Fatin, and his wife Lubna, were worried. They turned to a number of specialists and followed their advice, but to be on the safe side, they made a vow: once

Ayal starts speaking like any other child his age, they would slaughter a lamb and invite the entire family for a feast at Nabi Shueib. It is hard to tell what was more effective, the professional advice or the vow, but it is a fact that at the age of four, the child began talking, and he is now making up for the years of silence.

"Vows must be honored," said Ali Birani, "it took them several years, but eventually they invited the family for the feast, and I was, of course, very, very pleased."

Thus, the vows are not only a way of making wishes come true, but also a good opportunity—yet another good opportunity—for a large family reunion, accompanied by a delicious meal, of course.

Ali was all smiles watching his personal "tribe" surround him. True, similar gatherings would take place anywhere in the world, even in the usually smaller Western families. However, here, the very fact that the family celebration took place in the holiest of religious sites, gave this gathering an extra dimension.

I was almost envious. "Do you know why?" I asked our host. "I had no family. I was alone from the age of ten because of the war. Look how lucky you are."

* * *

With their unique outlook on life—this one and the next— Druze like Ali Birani and the Faraj family in Acre strive to balance their conservative traditions and values with contemporary demands. Their population is growing; they have taken modern professions, and they have earned the trust of the Jewish majority. However, they have also opened themselves to outside influences that are putting Druze solidarity—

and perseverance—to the test. The challenge is particularly demanding for the few Druze who leave their villages in favor of city life, like Dr. Janan Fallah-Faraj, the daughter of the first Druze judge in the country.

Janan and her husband Iyyad, a lawyer and an accountant, are the only Druze family in the mixed Jewish–Arab town. Theirs is one of the rare cases in which a Druze family chooses to leave the village. Naturally, they miss the warmth of the family in the village, but like many young couples in Israel, they too, could not resist the temptations of life in the city—and they evidently enjoy the affluence and comfort offered by their successful careers.

Janan Falah: "Yes, we still adhere to our tradition, but gradually, as we join the Israeli melting pot, our bonds might melt away. Don't forget, the Druze are a minority within a minority within a country that's a minority.

"I take my children to the villages during vacations, so they will know the whole family, their uncles and grandmother, so they are not cut off. This gives them strength."

Despite Janan's obvious dislike of religious conservatism, the family is not secular in the Western sense of the word. Both she and her husband accepted certain limitations, whose origin is religious but can also be viewed as adhering to tradition. Iyyad will not drink or smoke, nor will he allow Janan to go to the beach in a bathing suit—at least, not at home. In the French Riviera, why not? But not here, where a woman in a swimming suit will easily be the subject of ugly gossip. They may be the only Druze family living in the city, but they still spend weekends in the village. Most of their relatives and friends still live in the villages. The social pressure emanates from the village but does not stop at the city gates.

We mentioned the Riviera, because the family makes a

point of going abroad two or three times a year—always as a family: Iyyad, Janan, and their two boys Safi and Ghazi. Never alone. In the past, a Druze family with only two children was unknown. Janan, who comes from a family of six brothers and sisters, now considers having a third child. "My husband objects, let's see who wins."

As time passes, Druze villages seem to pull closer to the neighboring Jewish towns, whose influence on Druze youth grows stronger. High school graduates go to universities and colleges in the towns; teenagers spend free time at city malls, just like their Jewish counterparts, watching the girls go by, inhaling the consumerism of Western culture. They are slowly drifting away from old-time traditions. For better or worse, there is a world outside that is different from their traditional world, and its openness is often tempting.

That continuous tension between tradition and secularism troubles almost every Druze family. "I am afraid that modernism and the illusion that our youngsters can wear a bulletproof vest against negative alien influence will eventually kill our traditional values," said journalist Riad Ali of Mughar.

Although Riad did not serve in the army, his spacious house lies in the relatively new "veterans' neighborhood." It is a modern house, equipped with all the state-of-the-art electrical appliances, the latest laptop computer, and a car parked just outside. On the face of it, an ordinary, Western-style neighborhood. Riad warns, however, that this image is misleading. Unlike the villages on Mt. Carmel, home of families Birani and Mansour, which are close to the city of Haifa, Riad's village of Mughar is detached from large Jewish centers of population. The nearby town of Tiberias is a rather neglected semi-urban settlement, not quite attractive enough to pose real temptations to the young generation.

According to Riad's analysis, the Druze village was a ghetto of sorts, keeping the community united. Opening up to the outside world symbolizes a crack in the ghetto walls. The traditional segments in the society go on the defense. Riad believes that the Druze society is now undergoing a fundamentalist trend, very much like Jewish and Muslim repentants. "More and more girls who used to dress in modern Western attire return to the traditional Druze dress, covering their faces with a veil.

"We have what's called 'The Ninja's phenomenon'; women cover their faces fully, a custom adopted from the Islam, unfamiliar to the Druze community." It is, in Riad's view, a reflection of growing concern within the community of losing the links between past, present, and future, of fears that the common Druze family is not strong enough to cope with outside challenges.

"I am trying to educate my son as a Druze, but I feel that I am helpless vis-à-vis outside influence. More than at any other time in the past, we now need people of stature who can interpret religion in a modern way, but I don't see such people among our leaders. What we have today are either fundamentalists who drag us backward, or individuals who do not have the strength to pull us forward."

Given that the common Druze family is not equipped to do the job, in the absence of a decent leadership to show the way, the only real alternative is the education system. Alas, however, the educational system in Druze schools—very much like systems in the rest of the country—is rather mediocre. Most Druze teachers have neither the expertise nor the authority to fill in the growing gap in Druze heritage.

In an almost last-minute, emergency operation, Dr. Nissim Dana, that persistent observer of the Druze society in Israel, is now engaged in a project that should equip young Druze teachers with the tools to teach Druze heritage. The program includes Druze history and literature, as well as the basics of the Druze religion. Dana is convinced that the project stands a good chance of succeeding, because it meets a real need, for the first time engaging young Druze women teachers with academic education.

"Some members of the community feared that this was an attempt by the establishment to interfere in communal affairs," recounted Dana. "We needed to work hard to convince them that no one wants to break the framework."

The atmosphere is right to enlarge the Druze body of knowledge about themselves, said Dana. Contrary to fears voiced by many of the Druze with whom we spoke, Dana believes that mostly the community is not endangered and does not *feel* endangered. With opposition to the project virtually overcome, the challenge is for the young teachers to justify the hopes—against a multitude of odds.

Only two meetings in our Druze tour were held outside of a Druze village—the meeting with Janan Falah and her husband Iyyad, which was held in the town of Acre, and the meeting with Salman Natour, a writer and a poet, which was held in his office in Haifa.

Salman is truly a unique Druze. He is less attached to the community and more a man of the world—the Arab world, to be exact. His office is located in the predominantly Jewish city of Haifa, but it should be stressed that this does not mean that Salman is an integral part of the Israeli society. On the contrary, Natour, fluent in both Hebrew and Arabic, is the exception that proves the rule, a Druze who identifies himself as a Palestinian Arab and who states clearly, "I do not feel Israeli."

Natour heads the Emil Touma Institute for Palestinian and

Israeli Studies, located in an old Arab-style building in down-town Haifa. The late Touma was one of the leaders of the Israeli Communist Party. Salman Natour was at the time one of the young promises of the party, until he, too, broke away from the party of the God that failed. So now, with almost no funds available, Natour tries to steer the institute named after a Communist leader, away from Communism into the Israeli-Palestinian (mostly Palestinian) course.

Natour, a little on the heavy side, turning bald, and with two columns of gray hair on the edges, greets us in a large empty room in an empty apartment in the building—remnants of long-gone revolutionary glory. Druze heritage is just about the last subject the institute would deal with, but Salman seems quite happy to discuss the old roots. Yes, he is a proud Palestinian Arab, but talking to us, his Druze identity bursts out, almost in spite of himself.

Natour was born sixty years ago into a religious family in Daliat al-Carmel. His late father, Nayef, was a deeply religious person, as was his mother Ralia. He was one of eleven children: four boys and seven girls. The girls are all religious. Salman and two of his brothers proudly declare themselves secular Druze. Samih, the fourth brother, is a devout Druze.

He didn't just suddenly decide one day that he could not abide by the religious customs that his family had adopted. "It wasn't a switch; it was a process. I remember myself as a boy of fourteen at elementary school asking difficult questions about the basics of life, unable to accept religious answers. I found out that there is a world of wisdom where you can ask questions that, in the religious environment, you cannot ask. When I asked at home if there is God, my parents answered that this is a question that one cannot ask, because one cannot doubt the existence of

God. When I asked about the creation of the world, they stuck to the religious belief that the world was the creation of God."

Father Nayef accepted life as it is, as God had dictated it. If God wanted the Druze to be a minority in a Jewish state, so be it; let's make the best of it. Father Nayef, like most of the Druze of his generation and his children's generation, was well integrated into the Israeli society, working with Jews at the potash works at the Dead Sea, spending ten consecutive days at work, and then coming home to the village for five days.

Natour was already a philosophy student at the Hebrew University of Jerusalem when one day he came home and sat with his father until the middle of the night, asking all the questions he wasn't allowed to ask as a child. "I told him I reserved the right to doubt, but my father became very upset. He explained to me that religion was the intimate link between man and God, and every attempt to penetrate this intimate world is like peeping into the intimate world of a person. Finally he brushed me off, saying that I could believe whatever I wanted, but was sticking to his beliefs. On that day I decided that I would no longer argue with him, or with any religious people."

The fact that there was a "heretic" in the family did not mar the relations between the parents and their son. "This is a very tolerant religion; there is no religious coercion. Live and let live. The clergymen have failed to ban women from driving and to dictate their conservative dress code on Druze women. Nowadays, our girls enjoy greater freedom than in the past. If you visit a Druze village you see women wearing both religious and secular attire."

Salman's secular identity also molded his national identity. "I am a Palestinian Arab; my Druze identity is marginal. Of course, it is important for me what's happening to them, but this applies to everyone. I care for people. Precisely because my nonreligious and humanitarian identity, I cannot feel different from anyone else. I am glad that I was born into a very tolerant society, which does not affect my life whatsoever."

Salman is one of the few Druze who do not believe in reincarnation, that basic pillar of Druze religion and tradition. "It is a comforting belief," he concedes, "but deep inside I cannot accept it, unless proven otherwise." He doesn't believe in reincarnation, yet when he thinks of his father, who died in 1991, he doesn't count the years since his death, but rather since his rebirth. He, too, the secular rational poet, finds shelter from his bereavement in a belief that he does not actually share.

The belief in reincarnation, according to Natour, explains the introversion of Druze religion vis-à-vis others. Since Druze believe that a person's soul can be reincarnated only into another Druze's soul, there is no mixture of souls, and there is no intermarriage.

In yet another seemingly contradictory statement, however, Salman said, "We are not a closed society; nowadays we cannot be a closed society. Even in Me'ah She'arim, the ultraorthodox Jewish Haredi community in Jerusalem, the boundaries have been broken. Whatever happens in the West happens to us as well. Regardless of beautiful American values, what we get here is only American junk, because it is cheap and we believe that we cannot build a wall against it. But we must stand guard and protect ourselves against the negative influence of that culture."

Because Natour is free of any bondage to religion and tradition, it makes sense that he would have no reservations about whom his children—two boys and two girls—would marry. Well, not quite so. "I am never preoccupied with the thought of whom my children would marry. It is entirely their choice. All

I care about is the quality of the spouse. However, I understand that this is a process that must take place; there are no revolutions." It is therefore quite likely that even the children of Salman Natour, the "Palestinian Arab" will marry within their own Druze community.

Salman's beliefs in secularism and rationalism led him to Communism at an early age. "Although I haven't been a member of the Communist Party for the past fifteen years, I am still a Marxist. I believe that people should invest in changing their lives and that they should never accept life as it is."

Samih Natour, an observant Druze, offered an astounding figure. Only ten percent of the Druze consider themselves religious, he said. Actually, we expected a traditional society such as the Druze to be strictly religious. It turns out that the border between religion and tradition is quite blurred. Thus, even "secular" Druze try to observe the basic principles of Druze tradition. There is only so much "secularism" that one can take.

Samih is Salman's brother and his exact opposite. Salman is a secular Palestinian nationalist; Samih is a devout Druze, dressed like a man of religion. Relations between the two brothers are cool, a reflection of the tension in the community between the religious and the nonreligious. Both, incidentally, are men of letters: Salman is a well-known poet and writer; Samih runs his own publishing house. "We were raised in a religious house, but three of us did not become religious. This is not something exceptional. You can find both religious and secular people in the same family. We have no *kashrut* laws. Druze religion is both hard and comfortable. We believe in live and let live.

"Our religion preaches modesty, and our religious leaders are modest. When two religious leaders meet, they kiss each other's hand. Moreover, a true religious leader will insist on kissing the hand of the person who kissed him, because the entire religion is based on modesty."

Despite the low percentage of religious people, Natour agued that some sixty percent of the women are religious. Why? Because Druze women spend most of their time at home, where tradition is strongest and because women accept their role without dreams of seeking adventure elsewhere (or at least that's what most Druze men believe). Thus, said Samih, many women fulfill their lives through their religion. And those who do not think of themselves as very religious are still protective of the Druze traditions as a way of maintaining tribal solidarity.

People refer to the Druze religion as secretive. However, this is not quite the case, argues Samih. The basic commandments of the religion are open and well-known. The essence of the religion is so complex that one can explore it only through a deep study of the religion. This option, however, is open only to members of the Druze community. It is not an easy task to delve into the labyrinth of the Druze religion. "Only the great religious leaders really understand religion," said Samih.

SOUL SEARCHING

SIXTEEN MONTHS AFTER HE HAD been kidnapped by Palestinian gunmen in Gaza, Riad Ali, forty-four, is still a prisoner of his abductors. His body is here, in his comfortable living room in the village of Mughar, just minutes from the holy site of Nabi Shueib. His soul, however, is still very much there in that closed room in Gaza, where he was led to believe that he was living his last hours. Although he would want to "delete" that dark chapter in his life, his mind travels time and again to those inconceivable hours, unable to let go of them.

On the surface, he has recovered. He is married to his cousin Samia and has three lovely children, a girl Sabil, eight, a boy Luai, fourteen, and Ra'ed, eighteen, who will soon go into the army.

Ra'ed's enlistment, as well as Riad's personal trauma, have closed a circle. Riad Ali, whose national identity was as a Palestinian Arab, has changed identities. The "incident" taught him that, in time of need, only his Druze "tribe" and the Zionist state would come to his rescue. His eldest son was glad to join the army. Riad had managed to avoid the draft. The year was 1982: Israel had just invaded Lebanon, and the Druze community of Lebanon paid a heavy price for Israel's support of the Maronite Christian minority in that country. "Had there not been a war, I would have enlisted."

Riad is the black sheep of the family when it comes to the military. His father Sa'id was a career officer in the army, and his five brothers have all served in the army. Samia's brothers were all police and army officers. Riad worked as a journalist for CNN and Israeli Television Channel One. He spent years covering Palestinian affairs in the occupied territories. However, ever since the "incident," he has vowed never to cross the Green Line into the territories. He admits: "I am afraid. The trauma is still there."

We visited Riad at the end of our Druze tour to hear his analysis of the question at the core of what we had set out to explore: How does a traditional society cope with the changing times surrounded by an alien society? While we had been completely taken by how well the Druze had managed to maintain their identity so far, Riad shoved aside all the superlatives that we were heaping on the Druze.

"We are undergoing a crisis of modernization versus tradition, and the community is gradually realizing that it does not possess the religious tools to cope with the modernization. The secret nature of Druze religion, the absence of a religious establishment and religious ceremonies, combined with the fact that there is no religious indoctrination, have weakened the ties between the young generation and the religion.

"In the past, Druze identity was preserved because of outside threats—because at times they needed to live underground so as not to be harmed. This is one of the reasons they had kept their religion secret. However, ever since the establishment of the State of Israel, this pattern of self-preservation has been shattered. The Druze are no longer threatened as a community; military service gave youth the illusion of power. They no longer need to conceal their Druze identity, but rather be proud of it."

Unfortunately, whereas compulsory military service has given the Druze an admission ticket into the Israeli society, it has created a conflict with their own brethren in the neighboring countries of Lebanon and Syria. Walid Jumblatt, the leader of Lebanon's Druze has demanded repeatedly of his brethren in Israel not to serve in the army. Druze on the other side of the border have often accused their brethren in Israel of disloyalty to the Druze cause.

Riad believes that tradition has lost out in the conflict with modernization and military service for the simple reason that the Druze society has become so closely intertwined with another culture whose values clash so strongly with their own. Young Riad had no problem marrying his cousin Samia, accepting a more or less pre-arranged marriage. However, his son Ra'ed will most likely insist on freedom of choice in finding his partner in life. This, explained Riad, may seem perfectly progressive in the eyes of a Western observer. However, he said, it creates a certain embarrassment in the more conservative segments of the society. The young woman's father is keen on marrying off his daughter. If he cannot find a match, be it a cousin or anyone else, he'll feel as if he was dumping his daughter into the marketplace, exposing her to the community to be taken. What a shame, what a disgrace!

"This is a marketing process," said Riad, "marketing with emphasis on the package. Package means stressing the girl's attractiveness, modern dress, seductive appearance—elements that are so contradictory to the basic values of the community. Our society is still traditional; it cannot tolerate excessive interest in someone's daughter. You can look, but you cannot touch. However, the young men who have just returned from a three-year tour of the Western world come back home determined to check the product before they buy it.

"This tension is a formula for an explosion. Once a young couple wants to exercise their freedom of mutual choice, they face the well of communal tradition that does not allow the freedom of contact. Even today, extramarital relations are considered a crime that can be punishable by death."

This statement was rather shocking, coming from an educated Druze, a respected member of the press in Israel, the ultimate manifestation of progress and liberalism. It illustrated the wide gap between the traditional segments within the Druze society, and the new reality that was slowly encroaching on these isolated Druze villages. On the other hand, however, many parents now allow their daughters to go out to the city and study, thus expanding her horizons beyond that of homemaker. Nevertheless, at the same time, to use Riad's terminology—the matchmaking market is no longer limited to the village, but has expanded into the nearby cities. Thus yet another boundary of the close traditional society has been broken.

Riad's youngest child is only seven years old. There is still plenty of time before he has to worry about her, but the concern is there, setting off alarm bells that toll stronger and stronger as the years go by. "Suppose my daughter comes to me and says, 'I've fallen in love with a Jew.' What will I do? I hope that this will never happen. I know that the social price would be excommunication—and I don't want to pay it."

Why not, actually? Is that not a sort of racism? "I want her to marry a Druze, because I want to preserve my society. The preservation of my roots is part of my preservation as a Druze. Muslims and Christians are strong enough in numbers, so they do not care if they lose some members of the community. As long as you do not feel threatened, you have the privilege of breaking away from your natural framework."

This is the point where Druze illusion of power faces reality. "Within my own society, I have the illusion of power, but as I look around me, I feel threatened, just like the Jews. They feel strong vis-à-vis the Arabs in Israel, but as soon as they look outside they feel threatened. Secular and religious Jews may fight one another on the home front, but once they face a common enemy outside, they unite.

"Our existence as a group depends to a large degree on external pressure, just like the Jewish people. Thus, in a paradoxical way, the Druze community would have been much stronger had it not allied itself with the Jews. But that alliance is a fact, and I do not regret it. I feel lucky to have been given the opportunity to live side by side with the Jews—more as individuals than as a society."

So, what can the Druze do? "Family education can no longer carry the burden, because the father has pretty much lost the power he once had over his children. Now that family education can no longer do the job, the key to preserving the Druze identity is institutionalized education."

Riad Ali has pinpointed the problem. Israel's 115,000 Druze have been stuck at a crossroads for too long. They haven't quite decided—and agreed among themselves—how much they are Israeli, how much Arab, how much strictly Druze. "Young Druze ask questions," said Shimon Avivi. "They see that their Jewish and Arab neighbors have access to their Holy Scriptures, whereas because of their secret religion, only fifteen percent of them are exposed to religious answers to life. Many complain: We don't know what makes us Druze, because our scriptures are closed to us."

So, perhaps this is too difficult a challenge. Perhaps the present generation of young Druze need not force themselves to chose an identity. Perhaps they should work out a formula that would combine all, allowing them to live in peace with tradition and modernism, Jews and Palestinians, young and old. This is a challenge that needs a strong enough leadership to steer that beautiful and charming tribe between conflicting currents.

Does such leadership exist? Well, during the many interviews we conducted for the documentary, while the yearning for such a leadership was apparent, we didn't actually meet it. Perhaps this, too, is a price paid for this unusual encounter between a traditional society and outside challenges. Without a strong and visible external threat to combat, no real leaders have arisen.

Throughout our Druze tour through Druze society, we were fascinated by the Druze talent to maneuver between their two worlds, to see how they cope with a situation in which external temptations outdo external threats. Yet, despite all the admiration for the Druze we all developed for these people, we can't help but end this book with the note of warning issued by Ghassan Mansour, the accountant from Issfiya: "Compare our behavior today with that of ten years ago. It's like night and day. Twenty or thirty years from now, I think we will be so influenced by modernization that I am scared."

HISTORY IN A NUTSHELL

JUST AS THE DRUZE RELIGION itself is shrouded in mystery, the establishment of the Druze faith is also a bit murky. Some facts are widely accepted while others are not so clear. Even the very name *Druze* is likely to throw off anyone looking for the expected, as you will soon see. The Druze themselves didn't seem to think that historical facts were as important as discussions of religious and theological issues, and most of the Druze history about their formative years was written long after the events took place. The "facts" seem to depend somewhat on who is passing them on. Therefore, please do not look at this short history of the Druze as a hundred percent correct, but rather as a guide to give readers some idea of the origins of the Druze.

From the moment of the death of Mohammed, Muslims have been divided. Some believed that his successor should have been Mohammed's cousin and son-in-law, Ali ibn abi-Taleb, while others thought it should be his lieutenant, Abu-Bakr. The first group became what we call today Shiites, and the second became what are known today as Sunnis. Over the years there were many battles for power, with one side winning for a time and then the other. In 909 CE, there were two caliphs, or Muslim leaders, one Shiite and one Sunni. The Shiite Caliphate was called the Fatimid Dynasty; it soon covered all of North Africa, eventually extending into Syria and Palestine. It was under the Fatimids (named for Mohammed's daughter, Fatima) that the city of Cairo was built and from which the caliphs ruled.

The basis of the Druze religion is the belief that at various times God has been incarnated divinely in a living person, and that his last, and final such incarnation was al-Hakim (al-Hakim bi'amri-Allah, "the ruler in the name of God"), the sixth Fatimid caliph.

Al-Hakim was named caliph in 996 CE, though he was only eleven years old, and did not assume the reins of power until he was fourteen. It is difficult to characterize the man, as he seemed to have two sides. On one hand, he turned out to be a charismatic leader known for his honesty and reformist views. On the other hand, he showed little or no tolerance to those who had not followed his path, and was merciless and violent toward his opponents.

It is probably fitting that the Druze religion began under his reign, since he, too, was a man of complexities. Considered a true believer in the faith, al-Hakim lived modestly, just the opposite of the manner of the previous caliphs. He wore relatively simple clothes and is said to have ridden among his people on a donkey to ask them how they were doing. He freed slaves, banned polygamy, separated church and state, completed the al-Hakim mosque in Cairo, and improved the living conditions of the population by building hospitals and compensating people who lost everything in droughts or floods. Al-Hakim fostered science, art, and studies, and built the Dar al-Hikma (the Temple of Wisdom) in Cairo, the largest library in the world.

However, when elements of the population did not follow his example in the Muslim faith, he was not above using force and coercion to make them conform. Al-Hakim's brutality arose in response to what he considered debauchery and corruption in the courts of the caliphs of Baghdad, Damascus, and Halab. Money and women were in abundance among the ruling elite, while the rest of the population suffered from economic shortages, persecution, and scheming. As a result, al-Hakim took drastic action: He forbade all feminine activity in the courts, took away all women's rights, banned all public encounters between men and women, banned common bathing for men and women in public washing places, banned the manufacture and sale of alcohol, and punished thieves severely. Al-Hakim also prohibited the killing of cows, since they were needed for farming, ordered all dogs killed (except for hunting dogs), and decreed certain foods harmful.

While it is said that his mother was a Christian, it is al-Hakim who destroyed the Church of the Holy Sepulchre in Jerusalem (which covers the areas where Jesus is said to have been put on the cross and buried) along with three thousand other buildings. Moreover, it was because of his actions in the Holy Land that the Christian Crusades arose to reclaim Jerusalem. However, from our point of view, the important point is al-Hakim's contribution to the emergence of the Druze religion.

In 1016, an Iranian preacher, Muhammad bin Ismayil a-Darazi, went to Egypt. He offered his services to al-Hakim and was recruited to spread the beliefs of al-Hakim. But Darazi's beliefs, at least as stated, went beyond those of the Muslim faith. He believed in the transmigration of souls (reincarnation) and preached the divinity of al-Hakim. He must have been a good preacher, because he attracted many followers, whom their neighbors called "Druze." This name was "glued" to all followers of the new religion, although not all of them followed Darazi. Al-Hakim did not appreciate Darazi's rise to stardom. An inherently modest man, al-Hakim did not believe that he was a god, and felt that Darazi, in his sly manners, was trying to depict himself as a new prophet. Al-Hakim preferred another preacher, Hamza bin-Ali, over Darazi, and Darazi was executed. Hamza was now the sole leader of the new faith.

Though Darazi is not considered by the Druze to be a founder of their religion, their Muslim rivals purposely attached the name of the controversial preacher to the new sect, and it has stuck with them ever since.

It is believed that Hamza's writings on religion, which preached a type of unitarianism, form the basis of the Druze faith. (Remember the Druze sacred texts are kept secret, though some did fall into the hands of European libraries in the middle of the last century, though the Druze claim that they have been misinterpreted.) Regardless of whether Hamza considered al-Hakim to be divine while he was around, it seems that his view changed upon al-Hakim's disappearance. In 1021, al-Hakim went up into the mountains to pray, which was his habit, only this time he never returned, and his body was never found. One of the basics of the new religion is the belief that al-Hakim will return on the Day of Judgment.

The next caliph persecuted Hamza and his followers, and they were forced to go underground. The new Druze leader, Baha a-Din, moved the sect's activities from Cairo to the area now known as Lebanon, Syria, and northern Palestine, where they began to find new followers among the various tribes and a home for the Druze faith. Faced with a constant threat of persecution, however, a-Din declared in 1043 that only those current believers and their offspring could be considered Druze. The gates to the new religion were forcefully closed.

Establishing themselves as an exclusive and closed community of believers, the Druze soon improved their status with the Muslim rulers, playing a crucial role in the battles against the Crusaders. Druze leaders defeated Crusader forces in several important battles, including those in Aleppo in 1117, in Ra's al-Tinah in 1151, and in al-Damur in 1155. Saladin, the Kurdish warrior who overthrew the Fatimid dynasty to create his own Ayyoubi dynasty, joined forces with the Druze to defeat the Crusaders in the historic battle in Hittin, thus opening the way to win back Jerusalem later that year.

It was because of their contributions in these battles that the Druze first acquired their reputation as fierce fighters. Under the leadership of Sheikh Jamal a-Din Abdullah a-Tanoukhi (1417–1479), the Druze became a major regional force in the fifteenth century, enjoying a measure of independence.

In 1516, the Ottoman Empire was established, with Sultan Salim conquering Arab lands. He was supported by the Druze prince of Mt. Lebanon, Fakhr a-Din al-Ma'ani I, who reigned from 1506 to 1544. His son, Fakhr a-Din al-Ma'ani II advanced the Druze cause even further. The area prospered under his rule to the degree that the Ottomans felt their own rule threatened. Consequently, they assassinated Fakhr a-Din, just to be on the safe side.

From the sixteenth century until 1918, the Druze were under the nominal rule of Turkey, but they maintained virtual autonomy by their fierce opposition to any forces sent by the sultans to subjugate them.

In 1860, a bitter and bloody conflict broke out between the Druze and the Maronites (the Catholics in Syria and Lebanon). Thousands of Maronites were killed, scores of villages destroyed, and large numbers driven from their homes. However, although the Druze were victorious on the battlefield, they lost politically. European powers intervened to protect the Christians, and a French force occupied Lebanon for nearly a year. A Christian governor general was appointed administrator in 1864, and a large measure of autonomy was conferred on Lebanon, giving the Christians higher status than the Druze and the Muslims. These events marked the end of the political importance of the Druze in Lebanon.

Subsequently, thousands of Druze emigrated from Mt. Lebanon to the Horan region in south Syria, which soon acquired the name Jabel Druze, or Mt. Druze.

During World War I, most of the Druze remained neutral. However, when British ally Prince Faisal approached Damascus, an armed force of Syrian and Lebanese Druze helped him capture the ancient Syrian capital in October 1918.

As part of the post–World War I settlement, France received the mandate over Syria. At first, the French treated the Druze fairly, adopting the ancient principle of divide and rule, assuming that favorable relations with minorities would strengthen their grip against the Sunni majority in Syria. In the Druze congress in Swida on December 12, 1920, the French tolerated the proclamation of a Druze state in Syria. By April 1921, French Governor General Guru proclaimed the establishment of the first Druze government, under the presidency of Amir Salim al-Atrash. However, following the death of Amir Salim in 1923, the French appointed a French officer as governor of Jabel Druze, and relations between the Druze and the French authorities soon soured.

In April 1925, the Druze petitioned the French authorities for a hearing to discuss French breaches of the autonomy agreement. On July 11, 1925, General Maurice Sarrail, the high commissioner for the French mandate, ordered his delegate in Damascus to summon the Druze representatives. On arrival, the petitioners were seized and exiled by the French to the distant oasis of Palmyra, precipitating a Druze revolt that gave impetus to the independence struggles of Syria and Lebanon. Although the revolt was brutally suppressed, the Druze continued to enjoy a certain measure of autonomy until 1944, shortly before Syria's independence.

Ever since Lebanon gained independence in 1943, the Druze have maneuvered between the Christians and the Muslims to preserve their rights in a country whose constitution divided political powers between the Christians and the Muslims. Druze leader Walid Jumblatt is considered one of the more influential of those leaders. Following Israel's invasion of Lebanon in 1982, forces of Jumblatt's Progressive Socialist Party, armed with Syrian weapons, overran sixty Christian villages, killing thousands. This campaign was launched in response to attempts by the Maronite leadership—which felt it had the support of Israel—to ethnically cleanse Mt. Lebanon of its Druze inhabitants and in response to atrocities committed in the area. Jumblatt secured a Druze victory and solidified his position as leader of that community.

Jumblatt has a record of changing allegiances to ensure that the sectarian interests of the Druze emerge on the winning side. Like several other sectarian leaders, he supported the Syrian military presence in Lebanon after the civil war. However, ever since the death of former Syrian President Hafez al-Assad in 2000, and more so after the assassination of Lebanon's Premier Rafik Hariri in 2005, Jumblatt has become one of the strongest opponents of Syria, demanding their total withdrawal from Lebanon.

Today the status of the Druze people in the Middle East is quite stable. Devoid of national aspirations, the Druze enjoy a relatively high measure of security not only in Israel, but also in Syria and Lebanon. They are secure, but divided. For a community that regards brotherly mutual assistance as one of its prime pillars, the division between three enemy countries— Israel, Syria, and Lebanon—is a real burden. Political barriers

Druze young people harvesting olives on Mt. Carmel.

separate Druze brethren; closed borders prevent them from seeing each other.

On a hill outside the Israeli-controlled Golan village of Majdal Shams, local Druze occasionally gather to meet their relatives from Syria on the other side of the border fence.

They can see, but cannot touch. They cannot even approach the border fence too closely. So they stand there, watching their brethren on the other side of the hill and across the border, exchanging shouts through megaphones. It is called the shouting hill. They shout aloud, exchanging the latest family information, who was born, who got married, and who died, and whatever happened to Salman, who emigrated to the States, or to Rima, who crossed the border to marry a Syrian Druze and is already three-months pregnant.

They shout aloud. Only their voices are lucky enough to cross the border.

CONCLUSION

The Druze have managed to survive as a minority religion for so many years because of their ability to adapt to the cultures in which they lived. Now they face a crisis because the culture that surrounds them has adapted to them. How ironic it is that, because Israel is not trying to wipe out the Druze, the Israeli Druze are in grave danger of losing their identity. Ironically, it turns out that the risks of assimilation have turned out to be far more dangerous to this ancient religion and culture than are the risks of alienation.

This process of assimilation has flourished in the United States since the pilgrims landed at Plymouth Rock. However, it wasn't a problem, because the main body of whatever immigrants ended up being assimilated here resided back in the mother country. You might not be able to tell whether the person sitting next to you on the bus is Italian, Greek, or Spanish, but there are still plenty of Italians in Italy, Greeks in Greece, and Spaniards in Spain. There are Druze who live outside of Israel, but altogether the Druze population is minuscule, and to lose a significant portion would be a serious blow.

I won't try to predict what will happen. Certainly after making so many friends among the Israeli Druze I wish them a very long existence. But I will be following as closely as I can what happens to these people, and I urge you to do the same. The Druze offer us an example of what our world could be if only people weren't so stubborn. They've managed to maintain their values without trying to enforce them on anyone else. That is a lesson I wish others would heed. So keep your eye out for news about the Druze and if you ever get the opportunity to visit a Druze village, grab it. Then you'll see for yourself how hospitable and charming those people really are.

The Making of the Documentary

I've used the same crew to film several documentaries, with Michael Greenspan acting as writer and director and Colin Rosen as the cinematographer. These are great guys, and we love working together. Of course there are some difficulties. You see I am an impatient person. I get an idea to do a documentary, and I want it filmed and edited the very next day. Maybe even the very same day. But, of course, that can't happen. First I have to go about raising the money, and to do that I need a budget and written materials, which I want as soon as possible. Then I go around locating every source of funding imaginable, and the next thing you know I'm on the phone to Michael saying I'm coming over to Israel in two weeks; get ready to shoot. Many documentaries take years to prepare; mine take months. Michael and Colin bear the consequences of my impatience, but they also know enough not to cut any corners in order to produce the finished product, even if I am chomping at the bit. In the end, therefore, we make a great team and produce excellent films—if I do say so myself.

The one thing about making documentaries is that most of the time the subject you choose to cover is one that is not easy to get on film. That's natural, because audiences wouldn't be interested if you are showing them people and places that they can see every day. Moreover, I wouldn't be interested in making such a film. The main reason I do these documentaries is to learn something new myself. In the case of *The Olive and the Tree,* our job was to get ourselves into a community that is wide open to visitors on the surface and very closed just beneath that surface. Our key into this community was my coauthor, Gil Sedan. Having covered the Druze for many years as a journalist, and having always treated them with the utmost respect, he had trusted friends among the Druze. For example, with his aid, we were able to film a wedding ceremony that normally would have been open only to Druze, and were able to talk about religion with people who usually never talk about it. All of these contacts were, of course, equally helpful in writing this book.

I had a few contacts as well, and it was through them that we made inroads into the Israel Defense Forces. Looking at a map, one notices that Israel is a very narrow country that could be easily overrun. Politically, it is surrounded by enemies, therefore its armed forces are more important to Israel than those of any other country. As a result, the Israel government is quite secretive about their various armed forces and protect them from prying eyes. That we were able to shoot film of soldiers practicing with live ammunition was amazing. And the fact that we were able to speak to the first Druze to navigate an Israeli fighter jet was also quite a coup, because the Israeli Air Force is that country's most important asset. In the film, our Druze navigator wore his helmet and visor so that he would not be recognized, but no one tried to stop him from speaking his mind.

My favorite scene was when Michael had me sitting on top of a jeep to film some commentary. Part of the reason is that I'm short; I like it when I can look down at the camera. However, it also reminded me of when I was a member of the

Dr. Ruth on top of a jeep at a Druze unit with film crew.

Israeli underground (Haganah), making my contribution to Israel's independence. I know what it means to make a sacrifice for your people, which is why I so admire the Druze and wish them the very best in their efforts to maintain their culture.

About the Authors

Dr. Ruth K. Westheimer is best known for her pioneering work in the field of media psychology, specifically sex. However, her doctorate from Columbia University is in the Interdisciplinary Study of the Family, and she has created several books and documentary films investigating the family. The documentary on which the book is based, *The Olive and the Tree*, is airing on PBS stations across the country. She teaches seminars at both Yale and Princeton. Dr. Ruth is working on several new books to add to her collection of works about sex, and has a documentary on Bedouin women underway. This is her 32nd book.

Gil Sedan has worked for the past 30 years as Arab Affairs correspondent of Israel Television Channel One and the Jewish telegraphic Agency Jerusalem bureau. He's filmed documentaries on the Arab minority in Israel. Sedan was editor and host of the "Arabesque" Middle East television magazine, the only bilingual (Hebrew and Arabic) program in the region. Sedan has a major in History of the Middle East from Tel-Aviv University and M.A. in Journalism from the University of Missouri. He currently teaches television reporting in two colleges in northern Israel.